CAMPAIGN
for a
Better Life

20 Tools To Enrich Your Life and Everyone Around You

GARY BERGENSKE
Motivations

GARY BERGENSKE

Campaign For A Better Life by Gary Bergenske
Copyright © 2007 by Gary Bergenske
All Rights Reserved.
ISBN: 1-59755-118-X

Published by: ADVANTAGE BOOKS™
www.advbookstore.com

Library of Congress Control Number: 2007931688

Edited by; Le-Land E. A. Chase-Meadows of BEAUTIFUL MEDIA, Atlanta, GA

Photographs by; Jon Thomas Gumina of Jon Thomas Photography, Sanford, FL

Graphic design by; Jason Bergenske, Sanford, FL

Cover by Pat Theriault

First Printing: July 2007
07 08 09 10 11 12 13   10 9 8 7 6 5 4 3 2 1
Printed in the United States of America

Endorsements

"This book is a phenomenal encouragement for all of us! Gary Bergenske really simplifies the ways to build character, set your eyes on the prize and make your dreams become a reality! Superb!"

Bronson Kibler
Batteries Plus, LLC
National Account Sales Executive

An outstanding testament to **Gary Bergenske's** unparalleled leadership qualities! *Campaign For A Better Life* exudes a contagious energy, paving a road map to improving your life through character development, enthusiasm and integrity. Gary illustrates a realistic means to exceed your goals and maximize your potential.

Jason Leach
Careerbuilder.com, LLC
National Account Executive

Gary speaks to a way of life! Incredibly, Gary gets even better when he delivers his written word as a motivational speaker. He speaks and writes of underlying integrity and a positive attitude. Overcome adversity and achieve success at every level of your business, personal and spiritual life. – Transcending!

Thomas W. Storm
National Van Lines, Inc.
Account Executive

My good friend Gary Bergenske has shared many great thoughts and gives you the tools you need to improve yourself in ***Campaign for a Better Life***. Each chapter gives you a simple, easy to follow plan and is loaded with encouraging ideas. After years of knowing Gary, and working with him at the Shrine on his campaign, I'm excited he is sharing his excellent leadership knowledge in this book. This is an inspiring read and will change the rest of your life.

Happy Schuur
Crittenden Fruit Co., Inc.
Treasurer

Gary Bergenske's professionalism and leadership skills are reflected throughout this book that gives you the keys to improving your life. I recommend this book to everyone who wants to be a better leader. Gary has really put into perspective his better life plan. This is a book you will treasure and refer back to often. What a terrific benefit to all who want to excel in life.

John Seay
Retired Colonel
United States Army
Special Forces

"Not just another self-improvement manual, but an actual from-the-heart- plan for improving effectiveness in leadership and life…"

Katherine Phelps, Publisher
Beautiful Magazine

A must read for anyone wanting to be successful in life. Based on true life experiences, this book is very inspiring and instills excitement about building character! It demonstrates how to become a person of integrity.

Michael G. Juett
Skycraft Parts & Surplus, Inc.
Vice President / Owner

Motivations GARY BERGENSKE

Gary and Anne Bergenske in one of the promotional photos used in Gary's campaign for an international office with the Shriners.

Dedication

I dedicate this book to my wife Anne for her love, support, and understanding; and to our children, Carrie, Jami, Lisa, David, Jason, and Jared.

MAY GOD BLESS EACH OF THEM!

Gary Bergenske

TABLE OF CONTENTS

Foreword

In the local library or book store, you will find HOW TO books. How to cook in the Mandarin Chinese Style, Coach a basketball team, or How to have a better life. **Campaign for a Better Life**, is one man's semi-biographical journey to that better life. Many people search around in the dark to find that switch which turns on the light to a better life. The author believes he can help others find that switch.

Gary Bergenske believes the **Campaign for a Better Life** is fundamentally very simple. Make yourself a better person and you will be entering into a better life through leadership, family, and community. Your interaction with others is the basis of a better life. Success happens within this group.

The isolated man lacks the desire to be completely successful. Man, a social animal, to truly succeed must interact with others. The **Campaign for a Better Life** offers 20 tools to begin a journey of growth in leadership. Each section contains suggestions and examples to help guide you to that fulfillment. Principals and methods are shared that are easy to follow and will give you immediate results. After you read it, you will want to keep it handy as a daily reference or to share with friends.

Gary is active in his family's lives, the commercial community, and the Shriners of North America. A dedicated supporter of Shriners Hospitals for Children, he understands that only in leadership and in service to others is the better life. Through personal thoughts and examples the **Campaign for a Better Life** demonstrates HOW TO take those steps to make you a better person and in doing so living a life with greater quality.

Whether you wish to improve your life, become a more effective leader, or just to feel better about yourself, this is the book for you. A new focus will emerge in your thinking and that will touch your heart. This is all for the good. Sit down and begin reading, take notes, and then share with your friends. **It's all about a Campaign for a Better Life, yours.** When it come to improving your life, you can not go wrong. Read and enjoy............!

Pat Williams
Sr. Vice President, Orlando Magic
Author of over 40 books

Introduction

Very early in my life in Wisconsin, I learned if you wanted to get a good grade, play football, or in other words, succeed it required work, desire, focus, and commitment. I wasn't the best student, or the best football player but I approached every task with a commitment that no teacher or coach would ever say I didn't give my best. I graduated high school in 1972 and entered the workforce. There was no time to spend four years in college; I believed I could learn what I needed to succeed. I sold life insurance to put food on the table and a roof over my head.

For years sales was my business, but I had dreamed of owning my own business. I focused on my goal and went to work. Twelve years later in 1985 I bought, **J & J Metro**, a small moving and storage firm. I didn't know much about the moving and storage business, but knew it involved dealing with people, sales. Sales are communicating with others to sell a product, a service, or an idea. A company needs good employees to grow; therefore you must communicate as the leader or boss to your employees the benefits to all of hard work, good service.

The people of J & J Metro worked hard with me to grow and two years later we purchased a competitor, and then another, and another. With the help of my employees, the business will continue to grow. Success in business is only one part of life; there is success with a family, and the community.

With a good wife, Anne, and six children, I feel lucky to have a successful family life. As for community, I have my church, civic groups, and a volunteer fraternal organization, The Shriners. The Shriners are a group of men who wear funny hats and have a good time, but that is only a small part of the fraternity. The Shrine is devoted to service to the community.

Across the United States, Canada, and Mexico, there are 22 Shrine Hospitals for Children. The hospitals treat children with catastrophic burn injuries, orthopedic problems, and spinal cord injuries. There is no charge to any of these children's families because those men in the funny hats raise hundreds of millions of dollars to pay for construction and treatment.

The purpose of this book is to help you take a journey to improve your life. If you are serious about enriching your life, this is where you start. All the principals in this book can be applied to your personal life, church life, family life, or in your work place. The steps are there if you desire to commit the effort to make a better life.

You will find tools to unlock your mind and to inspire you to dream and carry those dreams to success. Chapters will help your self-improvement to help you develop the character of a true leader that others will respect. You will come to understand the importance of having a dream or goal. You will understand the power of a compliment or earned praise.

The book covers 20 important aspects for improving your life. Each section contains suggestions and examples to help guide you to that fulfillment. After you read it, you will want to keep it handy as a daily reference or to share with friends. It takes only you to make the commitment.

Whether you wish to improve your life, become a more effective leader, or just to feel better about yourself, you will enjoy this book. A new focus will emerge in your thinking and your heart will be touched. Sit down and begin reading, take notes, and then share with your friends. **It's all about YOUR Campaign for a Better Life.** When it comes to improving your life, this is an excellent place to start, you can not go wrong. Enjoy!

Gary Bergenske

Acknowledgements

I am grateful to Anne, my wife, for her support and help. She is my inspiration, a powerful influence, and my guiding light. Without her by my side and her belief in my dreams, this journey would not have been possible.

I thank my son, Jason, for all the hours and for his faithful dedication in designing the ShrinerGary.com web site that was the catalyst to write this book.

I'm extremely thankful to Le-Land E. A. Chase-Meadows of BEAUTIFUL MEDIA, Atlanta, GA who spent many hours editing. His professional talents are appreciated and have improved the quality of this book. I have enjoyed my experience working with him.

I acknowledge with deep appreciation all my friends and family whose aid made the writing of this book a reality. Your encouragement and input over the years allowed me to accumulate the information allowing me to improve my life. Now, I wrote this book to share the gift you gave me with everyone.

Gary Bergenske

Preface

Man is a social animal who gages his life by his relationships. First and foremost are his relationship with God and his family. Other associations have an equally important impact on our daily existence. I belong to The Ancient Arabic Order of Nobles of the Mystic Shrine for North American. This fraternal order and its charity, the Shriners Hospitals for Children, occupy a major part of my life. My family and the Shrine members of the Orlando, Florida area changed my life. Serving as Potentate during the 50th Anniversary of the Bahia Shriners in Orlando, I presided as The Central Florida Chapter generated an excitement and created an aura of community service that any volunteer organization could view with pride.

I have served the Shriners at the local and at the International level. Often my focus concerned increasing membership. All fraternal organizations strive to increase their active membership. I have had the opportunity to visit many Shrine Centers across North America to aid and assist them in day to day activities. Plans to grow membership and help the leaders evaluate their strengths and weaknesses of the local chapter were put in action. These tools helped them to focus on future goals.

After my year as Potentate, I decided to run for an International position. If I should win, a personal blessing would be in assisting the leadership of Shriners Hospitals for Children.

Campaigning for this position required travel across North America meeting Shriners at the 191 Shrine Centers. A vote held by elected representatives of each Shrine Center is held in July requiring a majority for election. If you win, you begin an eleven year journey that culminates as the top Shriner in the world.

In our travels, my wife and I have met wonderful people and seen beautiful places. The campaign included other venues such as mailings, phone conversations, and most importantly the support of the men and women of my campaign team. A new campaign tool involves the World Wide Web, but we decided the site had to be more than just "Vote for Gary", but should offer good solid information concerning the Shrine and its view of the future that would encourage return visits. With this in mind the www.ShrinerGary.com web site was born.

In the six month campaign, the site received over a half million hits, a true testament to the people of my team for which they can be proud. The July vote did not give me a victory, but it wasn't a defeat either. You can only be defeated if you quit. There will be another vote and another chance for victory.

Returning home from the vote, I visited the campaign web site. As I scanned the many stories and motivational ideas that had been accumulated, I realized that here was information beyond a simple campaign. Here were the guidelines for a **campaign for a better life** available for anyone. I made it a mission to take all this information and combine it in a book to offer insight and become a reference guide to the better life.

Life is queer with its twist and turns,
As every one of us sometimes learns,
And many a failure turns about,
When he might have won had he stuck it out,
Do not give up though the race seems slow,
You may succeed with another blow.

Success is failure turned inside out,
The silver tint of the clouds of doubt,
And you never can tell how close you are,
It may be near when it seems so far.
So stick to the fight when you're hardest hit,
It's when things seem worse,
That you must not quit.

Unknown

Chapter One can begin your **Campaign for a Better Life** if you want to expend the effort to start.

Gary J. Bergenske
Maitland, Florida
2007

"There is no such thing as <u>no chance</u>."

Henry Ford

Chapter One

A Positive Attitude For Life

Only You Can Control Your Attitude, Why Not Make It a Positive One?

Beginning your campaign for a better life, the place to start is with a positive attitude. Without a positive focus, what ever you attempt will not reach your expectations. A positive approach will open your mind to ideas and vistas to give you the ability and drive to perform at a high level day in and day out. Few people can consistently say they approach every task or challenge with positive thoughts. Winston Churchill said, *"Attitude is a little thing that makes a big difference."* History proves this one man's positive attitude gave the British people the will to resist in the face of seemly insurmountable odds. A positive attitude will make everything we talk about in this book happen more easily and with a better degree of success. A Positive attitude has been written about and talked about for numerous years and by many authors. Yet it seems to me, I know very few people who I can say consistently have one. A healthy attitude is contagious; but don't wait to catch it from others. ***Be a carrier.***

Attitude can be controlled, if you seriously commit to doing just that. Over the years, I have known people who remain focused despite all life's challenges. The ability to look at a problem realistically and then using their best resources to attack the task is the basis of a positive attitude. They diligently work the negatives out of the plan till all that remains is the positive. Some people are professionals at developing then keeping the positive attitude. It is evident in everything they attempt. The results are a successful life with many friends who admire and respect them. This is the best way to build you a better life. All challenges become smaller with the right attitude. I have heard the old cliché, "the harder I work, the luckier I get". I have said it myself, but thought the true meaning is, **"by keeping a good attitude, good things will happen for me."**

I pride myself in successfully keeping a positive mind regardless of the challenges I face. No matter how bad things appear, don't dwell on the negative; look for something good to accentuate the positive. Take the positive course by breaking the total problem into smaller pieces. The process may take time, but you may find you can solve one small part of the problem and that part will lead you to the key to begin building a total solution. All problems do not have a full solution, so you must take the partial victories and put the rest behind you, so you can move on with your positive attitude.

Situations rise and fall based on attitude. I've seen many times that successful people project a contagious positive attitude. As a result good things take place because they see the positive results before they even happen. This does not happen because they are positive, but being positive is a powerful tool in being prepared. Being positively prepared will bring with it good results. Life's successes are not determined by what happens in your life, but by the attitude you bring to life. As you look into the future, you must reach further. For the only way to find the limits of the possible is to travel into the impossible.

Education, ability, or stamina does not guarantee success, for I have seen a person with the right attitude triumph. The way you mentally consider the world as it presents itself around you marks your attitude. It is your view of the now and the future. One of my favorite stories I tell to put this attitude in perspective concerns an afternoon at a golf course.

Even though I am not much of a golfer, on an out of town business trip I visited a small local country club to play a round. After paying my green fees, I found a bench in the locker room to change into my golf shoes. As a stranger, you feel totally alone. As fate would have it, I sat next to a wonderful gentleman who struck up a conversation with me. Sometimes it takes only a few minutes of conversation for something magical to happen. Immediately, you feel as if you have known this person a lifetime. This happened to me as this man and I became very comfortable with each other.

Soon, we had our shoes on and headed for the door. I picked up my golf bag as did he. At that precise moment I said something that led to a lesson I will remember the rest of my life. I asked him,"are you going to play today?" You no doubt think what a silly thing to ask someone at a country club holding a bag of clubs. After I ask the question, I would have given almost anything to turn back the clock to give me the opportunity not to ask the question. However, the word spoken can never be recalled, so you must make the best of the mess you made.

The reason I asked was because the man had only one arm. We seemed to hit it off before and now I was certain I had hurt him and caused a rift in this new born friendship. Thankfully, he smiled and answered, "Please, don't feel bad. I get that question often, and it helps to motivate me." With his answer, I dared to ask the next natural question. "Just how good can you play with one arm?" He looked at me with a gleam of pride in his eyes. I knew I was about to get an answer I would love. His proud body demeanor told me I was about to receive a lesson I would remember for the rest of my life.

I listened as he slowly said, *"I've found on any given day, if I go out and play golf with my one arm and the right attitude, chances are I will beat anyone out there with two arms and the wrong attitude."*

What a statement. Let me repeat it.

> **"I have found that on any given day,**
> **If I go out and play golf with my one arm**
> **And the right attitude, chances are**
> **I will beat anyone out there with two arms**
> **And the wrong attitude."**

I remember this story and often think of it when my mind wonders in the wrong direction. Life is about making everything possible lean in your favor. Your attitude can be adjusted. Sometimes you have to say to yourself. "I can change my life by altering the attitude of my mind." You must make it positive to reap the benefits of building a better life. Remember, attitude is contagious. Is yours worth catching?

"People forget what you say,
And forget what you do, but forever
Remember how you make them feel!"

*"The best portion of a good man's life, -
His little nameless, unremembered acts
of kindness and love."*

William Wordsworth

Chapter Two

Having the Support
and
Love of Your Family

Their Support Can Help You Reach a Higher Goal

A lmost all the successful people in the world have a strong supportive family. A family that helps, supports, encourages, and dreams with them. A family's support can be the difference between success and failure. **There is nothing like sharing success with loved ones. Likewise, nothing compares with the love of a family in a time of failure or temporary set backs.** Having a family's support can be the key to keep you going when one feels like giving up. I have heard people Say, "It was because of my family that I kept going, I could never find a way to tell them I was quitting after all of the support they have given me. I love them so much; I could not let them down." It can be just that simple, success is found because you will not accept anything but the best.

If you have the support of your family and they share your dreams, success is much easier to accomplish. Personally, I believe my achievements are in a direct proportion to the support I have received from my family. In my business and personal life the support of my wife and children is paramount to the way I work. Without family would be an empty trip hardly worth traveling.

Building unconditional family support and love takes a constant commitment from each family member. Support and love begins with respect. Respect for the individual, for their ideas, their needs, and their dreams. Believing in each other is next, as that belief is what empowers one to do more.

Believing In Each Other Gives Them the Fuel to Live Their Dreams to the Fullest.

Follow these qualities with affection, family time, concern for each others well being, good communications, and the sense to allow the individual time and space. Each area can be expanded but it is important to include them in your formula to create a tight knit family. Remember different family members excel in varied disciplines. Don't try to force a family member into your mold. Respect individual character, it is what makes them special. This is especially true in children. This accentuates love and support which builds solid family relationships.

When I decided that my dream was to run for an International office in the Shriners, I knew my first task was to get my family's blessing. For the first time in my life, I felt I needed their unconditional support for this long range goal. It would put my family's support to the test.

The primary support would have to come from Anne, my wife. She understood how deeply important this ambition was to me. Once I had her commitment to support my intentions everything looked easier. I knew her support would mean sacrifices on her part, and that made it all the more important to me.

Her devotion to my dream required travel throughout North America. This meant she would have less time with the children and grandchildren. Her vacation time would become moot. I felt this was a true sign of her love for me. When I asked how I was so fortunate in having her support, she answered immediately, **"I know how important it is to you; I'm here to help you if I can."** I knew her response came from the core values within the family.

Her Love and Support Came From The Core Values Within Our Family

Having Anne as part of my team helped immensely. She always has been an asset to me. Her genuine and gracious nature coupled with excellent people skills always represents me in the highest fashion. I often joke that when she is with me, I look good. I would never have dared to think of entering the campaign without her and her support.

I sought my mother's support because we have a close relationship especially since my father died. I could not imagine taking on this challenge without asking her opinion. I have always counted on her support. Just the fact she knew of my plans helped me. Her continued faithful positive support for me inspires me to do more than I thought I could.

Family Love and Support Can Move From Generation To Generation

That left the children, this would be a test of all Anne and I had taught the children about family values, support, and love. I tried to talk to each one individually and was happy when they offered to help as I needed. They were giving back what Anne and I had always attempted to instill in their family values. It gave me the strength I needed to feel good about myself, as my family was fully behind me. I knew that what I was doing had to be right. It also made me realize how family love and support can move from generation to generation

Going through this made our family stronger. With one of our daughters, Jami and her husband Jason; it was a walk on the beach as I told them about my dream. They were totally supportive. They respected my dream, and encouraged me regularly.

Our oldest daughter Carrie said this about family. "I think that is what family is for...to be there...to support us...even when it takes lots of sacrifice. Family is there to help, to encourage, to believe, in a world where others try to tear us down. Family gives us the courage and the strength to follow through with our dreams." She also said, "Families need lots of unconditional love, support, forgiveness, team work, encouragement, truth, communication, these are the things that make a great family." I really began to feel great about the tools my family was using.

Family Gives Us the Courage And The Strength to Follow Through With Our Dreams And Often Requires Sacrifices

My daughter in-law Jane had this to say about family love and support; "Sometimes we feel obligated to support or help another family member. When a person, especially a parent has supported us, we do not feel obligated to support them; we feel we want to support them. The support of a family stems from the parents themselves. When they encourage greatness and give positive support for everything a child does, even when something goes wrong. In return a child will also encourage greatness and positive support back to their parents and family. **It becomes a cycle of _wanting_ to support each other**."

If you want to know what kind of family you have, listen to the young children. Another test is how your teenagers describes your family to one of their friends. Building family respect is an everyday job that never ends, but it is rewarding.

Building Family Respect is an Everyday Job that Never Quits.

Several years ago, I received a letter from Lisa, one of my daughters. It was a short letter, only a single page, written shortly after her high school senior year. An exciting time in her life, she prepared to leave the family nest and enter university life. Recently, I found it and it brought tears to my eyes. I would like to share the last paragraph of the letter.

> *"One last thing before I close Dad. I just wanted to let you know that some of the most meaningful things that you have ever given me were those personalized letters that contained poems and inspiration in my Christmas card, Graduation card, and a few others. You are very good at writing from the heart. Those letters to this day are hanging in my closet and I read them once in a while. Sometimes my friends even read them. Those letters I will treasure for the rest of my life. You are so sweet. Thank you for being you. I love you."* **Lisa**

It is often difficult for us to see the effect small things like my notes, cards, or Lisa's letter has on our lives. But it is just these small acts of kindness or love that build larger relationships. I have tried to set a good example in my family life, my business dealings, and my community. Often we never see if we have any effect.

After two serious automobile accidents, either of which could have been fatal, I saw an example of character and heart in my own daughter. Working through physical pain to regain her athletic abilities, Lisa used that very struggle to excel at her university studies. The culmination of her efforts resulted in her graduating from Warner Southern University at the top of her class and being elected captain of the women's basketball team.

I could search thorough volumes of biographies, but I do not think I could find a better example of courage, character, or perseverance than my daughter, Lisa. She is married and expecting her first child. I am certain she will be a good example to her children. It is my profound hope my example to her reflects in small part the character Lisa displays. It is by example that we help others grow in character.

Just as she treasures my notes, I treasure hers. It is the mutual give and take that makes the family unit work together and support each other. Wither you seek an office or campaign for a better life, your family is an important facet to your success. Love, respect and believe in them. On the next page is a note I wrote to encourage my children to dream. I have used it often in my presentations:

"Make Your Dreams Happen"

Always remember,
If you can dream it,
It is often possible.
As you go through life,
You will find that making your dreams
Come true can be some of the most
Rewarding experiences in your life.
Many dreams can and do come true
If you believe.
Go out on to the World and
"Make your Dreams Happen"
It will give you the
Greatest feeling.

Chapter Three

Focused Leadership Ability

Qualities of a True Leader
20 Key Points to Get You Where You Want to Go

"The task of the leader is to get his People from where they are to where They have not been,"
Henry Kissinger

S uccessful leaders have certain characteristics that are common among them. You could believe a recipe exist that you could mix a bit of talent, a pinch of vision, a teaspoon of drive, a cup of personality, then heat with a challenge, and voila you have a leader. To a point this is true;

leaders are developed and trained to become successful. Setting achievable goals and then following through to completion are the building blocks for a successful leader. Leaders continually work to make themselves and their people skills better by accepting greater and greater challenges. Good leaders are never satisfied with their level of achievement; but push to raise their abilities. By example, they impact the lives of all around them. The feeling of making a difference is both their reward and the urge to continue to lead.

Everyone is offered the opportunity to become a good leader. A person must have the desire and be willing to become a student of leadership. Leaders always want to learn more, they possess the hunger to learn the skills needed to improve.

Communication is the key. Good leaders communicate with the group. The word communicate presupposes two directions. The leader clearly defines their vision and then listens. By bringing everyone into the planning stage, the leader excites the group. The first step is always the responsibility of the leader. **Leading by example is, indeed, one of the most important aspects of leadership.** Another prime example of good leadership is the talent to recognize strengths in others, and then to delegate authority. Most communal tasks are too large for a single person, so another aspect of leadership is the ability to divide the task and assign another person to perform it. This does not mean the leader is above anyone. Individuals are recognized as leaders due to their actions. A good leader must be willing to get his hands dirty with any task. You will gain in respect and support by participating at the working level. Letting others understand that you will work on any task no matter how small will go a long way in garnering respect and promoting positive conduct. Motivation feeds off motivation. A leader uses his motivation to arouse others to a higher performance. A great leader is one who makes every person in the group feel as if they will deliver a part and may even deliver the part that insures the final success. Simply, a great leader leads by instilling in the individual a desire for the group to triumph.

Ralph Waldo Emerson wrote, *"A great man is willing to be little."*

Leaders believe in themselves and that everyone surrounding them has the capabilities to higher accomplishments. A true leader makes people realize their full potential and how to inspire them to further effort. Jerry Kramer a former Green Bay Packer player who played in Super Bowls 1 and 2 and has become a well known sports author spoke of the leadership of Vince Lombardi said, *"He made us better than we thought we could be."* This is the sign of a truly great leader.

Great leaders have uncanny belief and vision. They are willing to do whatever it takes to make a project successful. Leaders never stop believing in themselves or their associates. Belief is the inner feeling that when ever we undertake a task, we can complete it. For the most part, we each have the ability to look at a task and see if it is within our powers. The leader's job is to open eyes to the possibility that we may reach beyond our perceived abilities and attain a higher vision. Believing is the key to achieving and it is contagious.

A leader creates motivation in himself and in others. Through his commitment, desire, drive, and sacrifice others are inspired and motivated to help and do their part.

Leadership qualities continue to grow through education, responding to change, and setting of goals. Setting a goal will give clear objectives and motivations to continue leading. I repeat, true leaders are not born, but are developed by individuals who possess the want and desire to dedicate themselves to becoming a leader. The decision is yours, what kind of a leader do you want to become?

In my campaign to be elected to an International office, I felt I needed to come up with clear descriptions of what I believed a true leader should represent. I researched sources and talked to numerous people on what they thought it takes to become and remain a good leader. This would formulate the guidelines and rules I needed to live by if I were to be recognized as a leader.

Leadership Qualities

1. Leaders need a clear vision of where they wish to go. They do not keep their vision secret, but share it in the hope of mobilizing their associates to move in the same direction.

2. Leaders are consistent. They remain true to their principles and values.

3. Leaders do what they expect of others. They "walk the talk"

4. Leaders are good communicators, who focus on delivering their message.

5. Leaders are not threatened by other's competence. They surround themselves with outstanding peers who energize them.

6. Leaders look for and recognize superior performance and are quick to give credit and praise to the individual, his family, and to publish it to others who should know.

7. Leaders enjoy seeing others increase their skills and confidence. They share their knowledge to assist colleagues to accept greater challenges and responsibilities.

8. Leaders don't betray trust, they honor it. They treat confidential information professionally.

9. Leaders are concerned with positive outcome and refuse to become embroiled in negative political infighting. They encourage those around them to do likewise.

10. Leaders confront issues in a timely manner even if it is uncomfortable. Procrastination or putting problems aside only leads to further difficulties later.

11. Leaders are flexible and adapt to change. They see modernization as an opportunity rather than a threat. They do not remain in an old position or tradition simply because it is more comfortable.

12. Leaders are human. They make mistakes, and when it happens they openly admit it.

13. Leaders learn from their mistakes. They use errors as guides to improve their skills. A mistake is used as a catalyst to renew your energy.

14. Leaders enjoy the challenge and are willing to take risk and encourage others to do the same. Failure becomes a learning exercise on the path to success.

15. Leaders focus on the future not the past. They anticipate trends and prepare for them.

16. Leaders encourage and reward cooperation within and between teams. They are supporters of teamwork, as it makes all work more productive.

17. Leaders develop guidelines and goals for the team. They expand the guidelines as the team becomes willing to accept more responsibility and raise their goals.

18. Leaders change their role according to the needs of the team. They are ready to step aside and become a mentor or facilitator if needed.

19. Leaders listen. The second part of communication is listening to fellow team members. They respect others and allow themselves to be influenced for the good of teamwork.

20. Leaders consistently involve others in finding new ways to achieve goals. Lists of all goals should be written and regularly updated. The goals must be measurable.

The true value of a leader is not judged while serving, but it is determined by how those he has influenced perform once he is no longer there.

Chapter Four

Contagious Energy

Developing Enthusiasm in All Aspect of Your Life

"Energy and persistence conquer all things."
Benjamin Franklin

I stand in front of my seat at an ***Orlando Magic*** Home Playoff game. The unbelievable noise is so loud it is impossible to talk to the person next to you. Your eyes travel all over the arena during a time out. The Magic Dancers shake on the court as Stuff the Magic Dragon, the Magic mascot, walks on the courtside tables. Streamers and balloons fly around the arena. The energy and enthusiasm is at an all time high. This is a point of no return; the atmosphere is so contagious you could not leave even if you wanted. Each and every person in the stadium is standing waving their arms and yelling at the top of their lungs.

Time out is over. The noise remains so loud there is no way to hear the official's whistle. Despite the noise, somehow the Chicago Bull players line up to inbound the ball. There is no surprise; the ball is inbounded to Michael Jordan. With a full court to go, he dribbles over the center line. Though I would not have believed it, the noise volume actually increased. The contagious energy in the arena is beyond belief.

Jordan glides smoothly down the sideline, with his usual expertise, towards the three point line. Appearing out of nowhere, Magic's Nick Anderson slips behind to steal the ball from the league's premier player with only seconds left on the clock. The crowd goes absolutely crazy. It becomes a moment you will never forget. **Unbelievable excitement with a contagious, enthusiastic energy, the magnitude is impossible to express, you actually had to feel it as a participant.** To fully appreciate the moment, you had to be there.

If you could bring this type of contagious energy to your workplace, home, or volunteer organization, it would be great. However, that level of mayhem is best left in the arenas. But contagious, enthusiastic energy has its place in every successful person's life. The key to unlock that type of energy is desire. It grows and radiates from you till it begins to capture the interest of others. It then becomes contagious passing from one person to the next. If you have that zest of enthusiasm, you will attract others that have the same belief. Together as a group it will become so contagious others will want to join. *Have you ever met an enthusiastic person who was not contagious?* Enthusiasm engages people; it brings them to see what all the excitement is about.

To be enthusiastic, you must believe in what you are doing totally. You must love what you do and do what you love to be really enthusiastic. The more energetic you are, the more effective you will become. If you believe in your plan or dream, your body language will present itself in an enthusiastic and high energy manner. You will become contagious in your endeavor of attracting others who will want to join and help. Soon you will be producing positive results.

If you consider history, no great event ever happened without a tremendous amount of enthusiasm. The Renaissance, revolutions, the machine age, or now the information age are the children of man's enthusiasm. Small changes and projects have their beginnings with enthusiasm. It is the real energy, the magical influence that makes the difference between mediocrity and amazing success. The world's greatest success stories concern people who struggled forward to a successful outcome, when the rest of the world thought it impossible. A true leader is full of energy and vision. He combines those traits with a plan executed with enthusiasm to bring about a positive, contagious result. Wow, is that a mouthful, but it is so true.

A cheerleader without enthusiasm would be just another unexcited fan. The football player that lacks enthusiasm would not even make a good water boy. Without enthusiasm, a salesman would be no more than a clerk. **Energy and contagious enthusiasm make things happen, it is as simple as that.** When times get tough, it is essential you keep your enthusiasm for others to see. Abraham Lincoln said, **"Success is going from failure to failure without losing**

your enthusiasm." Mood affects the manner you present yourself, which in turn reflects your body language. An essential part of promoting yourself, your business, and your beliefs is staying positive and enthusiastic.

As you **campaign for a better life,** it is essential you maintain a contagious enthusiasm to increase your chances for success. According to recent Gallup studies a widely recognized barometer of American opinion that only approximately 15% of American workers are doing their very best at their jobs. Another 10% are burned out. That means the final 75% do just enough to get by. These 75% live from pay check to pay check with little chance of bettering themselves. Why? These are the ones who lack everything that I have been writing about. They have little drive or energy and can find nothing to be enthusiastic about. This blinds them from having vision or hope of achieving a better life. Imagine how productivity would soar if all these people were enthusiastic about their jobs. A new found energy would be born lifting America to new heights by improving morale, job retention, and industrial productivity therein guaranteeing our citizens to an enriched life. In a 24 hour day you spend time at work, at home, and at sleep. Because a job occupies a third of your life, it is important not to waste this valuable time. Find a way to become enthusiastic about work. If you do, you'll find enthusiasm in all the other parts of your life. That will put a *"touch of splendor"* in everything.

Enthusiasm is not built by wishing. Only passion and love of what you are doing can affect enthusiasm. Starting with one person it will spread through an entire organization or team. Do you want to be an igniter of contagious enthusiasm? Begin with positive statements about the task, and then your energy and infectious attitude will spread from one person to another. **"Enthusiasm,"** according to Henry Ford, **"is the yeast that makes your hopes shine to the stars. Enthusiasm is the sparkle in your eyes, the swing of your gait. The grip of your hand, the irresistible surge of will and energy to execute your ideas."**

Generating enthusiasm can be intentionally planned, if the details are worked out in advance of the event. College football is an excellent example. Pep rallies, bands playing, cheerleaders flinging cheerleaders, and the team mascots prancing around the field. Their mission is to excite your interest and build involvement and enthusiasm in the game. By kickoff the energy and enthusiasm should be contagious throughout the stadium.

In my personal experience of attending meetings or seminars, the enthusiasm in a gathering can intensify or wane based on the attitude, delivery, and energy of the presenter. An enthusiastic speaker is contagious; likewise if he is boring you might fall asleep. Enthusiasm cultivated, nurtured, and spread by someone who takes up the challenge through showing a passionate interest and an eagerness to share with others.

Using unexpected details to catch the attention of others begins the process of generating enthusiasm. If it is genuine, it will be infectious passing from one person to the next. Spreading from person to person, company to company, or nation to nation, enthusiasm is limitless. In ancient times, wars were put on hold for the warring parties to participate in the Olympic Games. Enthusiasm for the sporting events eclipsed war.

You can light the torch of enthusiasm. It starts within you. By sharing your ardor and passion, you will make a difference in the attitude of those that surround you.

You Can Light the Torch of Enthusiasm
It Starts Within You

Earlier, I cited an example of how 17,000 people at a NBA Playoff exploded with contagious energy. Now, let me share a story of a man who possessed the enthusiasm and energy to make his childhood dream reality. It didn't matter what others said, he remained true to his desire and made it happen.

He Always Wanted To Fly, That Was His Dream
Since He Was a Little Boy

This is a true story about a man, Larry Walters, who always wanted to fly. He dreamed of flying since he was a little boy. The Air Force seemed to be his answer, but he failed the eye examination to enter pilot training. After fulfilling his military obligation, he became a truck driver in southern California, but never stopped dreaming of flight. One afternoon sitting in a lawn chair in his North Hollywood backyard, he watched the white jet contrails crisscross the purple blue California sky. Larry began to plan. Visiting his local Army-Navy surplus store, he purchased 45 weather balloons. Now, these were not your average party balloons; these balloons measured six feet in diameter. The first step in his plan was complete with the purchase of several tanks of helium.

It's July 2nd, 1982, X day. Arranged across Larry's back yard are the balloons each tied with cord that is attached to the comfortable lawn chair. The chair secured to the bumper of Larry's jeep by a heavy canvas cord awaits the moment of flight. Now, the adventure begins. As each balloon inflates it rises to take place among its cousins in tiers. With all 45 balloons straining at their tethers, Larry returned to make a sack lunch for his journey. Wearing his parachute Larry walked back to his favorite chair. He carried his son's BB gun that he planned to regulate his altitude by shooting the balloons one at a time.

Sitting in the chair, Larry begins his count down. He reaches down to cut the tether to the Jeep expecting to float lazily up into the air. No one seeing his lift off would describe it as lazily floating upward. In fact Larry is flung skyward like he had been shot from the cannon at the Shrine Circus. His astronomical rise only slows as he reached 16,000 feet. Now, the reason we know this is a pilot for Delta Airline on his approach to LAX reported to the tower, "You are not going to believe this but there's a guy outside my port window in a lawn chair with a rifle in his lap." He was right, they didn't believe him. You might think the tower personnel thought the flight attendants were serving cocktails in the pilot's cabin. After a time, they believed. So, did the local television news people. Others became interested as the news spread. Primary among these interested parties were the police and the FBI. Larry's little journey into the flight path of air traffic created a major stir. By the time he reached mother earth again, the police waited to cuff him.

The police not sure of what the charge would be decided to arrest him and let someone else sort it out later. During a lunch with a friend who was a pilot, I told him the story. He said, "The usual punishment for someone who interferes with the airspace at an airport would be the loss of the pilot's license." Larry didn't have a pilot license, but the police knew they had to arrest him. As the police carted Larry away, a reporter managed to ask, "Mr. Walters, why did you do it? Larry said without hesitation, "A man just can't sit around doin' nuthin'." I love that. ***"A man just can't sit around doin' nuthin'."***

The enthusiasm for a dream was demonstrated by his desire and the energy Larry put forth to make it a reality. If all of us work with this type of commitment, the world would be different. Make your dreams a reality, and do it with contagious, enthusiastic energy. If you do, others will want to be part of your team.

President John F. Kennedy said this about energy in his inaugural address, January 20th, 1961 in regards to where Americans were in the world:

> *"I do not believe that any of us would exchange places with any other people or any other generation. The energy, the faith, the devotion which we bring to this endeavor will light our country and all who serve it, and the glow from that fire can truly light the world. And so, my fellow Americans: ask not what your country can do for you – ask what you can do for your country."*

"A man can succeed at almost anything
For which he has unlimited enthusiasm."
Author Unknown

Chapter Five

Character With Integrity

Build Yours and People Will Respect You

"I do the very best I know how – The very best I can; and I mean to keep on doing so until the end." **Abraham Lincoln**

C haracter has many faces and many meanings. Webster's defines it as: (1) the aggregate of features and traits that form the individual nature of a person or thing. (2) moral or ethical quality, (3) qualities of honesty, fortitude, etc.; integrity. The definition continues for another page; but it really means, **who you really are.** Character like leadership is not born in you; it is taught, developed, and maintained by you. Every person builds their own character. Ability can take you to the top, but it is character that keeps you there.

There are all types of characters, from good ones to bad ones, quiet ones to flamboyant ones, eccentric to conventional. If I were to choose what I believe to be the highest level of character, I could define it in one word, **integrity**. Integrity means adhering to the highest moral principals and professional standards. Living as one with this type of character will reap the rewards of respect from your peers. The highest qualities of character can be acquired in only one way, they must be earned.

As you go through life, the choices made and the manner we handle the good times and the bad that we experience reflect our character. How you as an individual respond to the never ending challenges of life will determine your character. You are responsible to build it in the right direction. A character founded on integrity should be your goal to acquire a successful, prosperous, and rewarding life. Your reputation is what others think of you, but character is who you really are in fact. What you do, when you alone would know the right or wrong of your actions, is the true test of ones character.

How do you build a character that garners respect? **Character is not about having everyone like you; it's about making everyone respect you and for what you stand.** It is about making the right moral decisions based on the highest values, ethics, and professional standards. True character is in the disciplined day to day habit of doing right even when it is not the easiest or most popular thing to do.

In the world today, there are people who have allowed their character to be tarnished. People have sold themselves through dishonesty, unfaithfulness, and in making bad decisions. Some have given up the one thing they should hold most precious and never let be taken from them, their good character. There are rules of conduct practiced over your lifetime that aid in building good character. In my life, I have found 10 principals, which formed for me a roadmap to having a character others can respect.

I believe if you are to build character that others respect and look to you for leadership and advice, you must work at it everyday. It takes years to build a character worthy of respect, but only moments to destroy it. A person who values his integrity does so ALL the time, not at just selected intervals.

To Have the Character of a True Leader It Takes Years to Build and Only Moments to Destroy

Consider making the following 10 points as part of your everyday life to build character...for life. Take the challenge and begin today to build your character. Your good character is more likely to be praised than your talents. Most talents are to some extent, a gift. Good character, by contrast, is not given to us. We build it piece by piece—thought by thought. The right choices, coupled with courage and determination will soon show your true character.

Ten Character Builders

Live with Integrity: Devoting your existence to living a life filled with the quality of possessing and adhering to the highest of professional standards.

Practice Good Ethics: The established habit of performing desired principles governed by your appropriate conduct, to be of high quality and to live decently and honorably.

Respect Others: Treats all people with dignity. Works to show thoughtfulness, and to feel or show admiration. Looks for the best in others and will value their opinions.

Positive Qualities: The art of producing good results by having an innately beneficial character that thrives on excellence and high standards.

Moral Mind: Able to act on the principles of right and wrong as they govern the standards of premier behavior. Is self guided on how to act decently and respectably.

Behave Honorably: To act in an impeccable way, especially by being polite, good-tempered, and self-controlled. Develops a reputation of living by strong moral and ethical principles.

Honest to All: Truthful, true and unbiased. Is a sincere, straightforward, law-abiding citizen who considers all situations in an impartial way.

Decent Always: Kind, considerate, well-mannered, and generous. Constantly conforms to accepted standards of proper moral behavior on every occasion.

Sets an Example: Lives a life that illustrates a model of exemplar behavior worthy of being copied or imitated. Inspires others through irrefutable conduct.

Good Conscience: The internal sense of governing your thoughts and actions by allowing your core values to be your guide for what is fair and reasonable.

A person of good character can come from any race, religion, or country and is not confined to any one economic level. The only common denominator among those with a character of integrity is in their core values. It comes from inside of us, from our heart and soul. Core values are built from truth, a continued persistent search for excellence, and a willingness to do right in spite of pressure to do otherwise.

What guides you to your core values? **Values are determined by what you personally decide is acceptable to you and what is not acceptable.** It sounds simple, but to find the answer will involve real soul searching. Think about it, everything we do in life has guides. The clock on the wall directs our comings and going during the day. In golf, the fairways guide us to the green. Gutters on either side of the alley mark the limitations for the bowling ball. If we drive an automobile, we use a map, or the traffic signals and the white lines on the pavement as guides. How are you guided by character? Believe it or not, your core values are the guidance for character. Want to know what are your core values? Answer these few questions to begin to get a handle on them.

What adjectives describe your life?

If you were to die today, what would others remember about you?

What am I doing that I can be proudest of in my life?

What would I be willing to die for?

What would I put in a letter to my children about what is important to me?

What one word would you want on your tombstone?

After answering these questions, what do you think about your core values? Your character? Evaluate your guides, and then fill your life with good values and they will begin to set the character of who you are. Write down your family's values, your personal values, and your business values. Do they align? When your core values improve then your character will be one of integrity.

Unlike your fingerprints, character is not something with which you are born, without a chance to alter and improve. **Every individual is charged with the responsibility of building and forming their own character.** Much is said about the environment in which a child is raised in determining the child's character. But even the best parents can not guarantee their child's good character. Good character results from the relentless pursuit of living a life built on good values.

I like what President Abraham Lincoln said about the test of a man's character. **"Nearly all men can stand adversity, but if you want to test a man's character, give him power."** I have found this to be true. Priorities must remain in focus at all times, regardless of your position. If you do not live by this, then your character will begin to change, and it will not change for the good. I have seen men work hard to reach higher positions, positions with more responsibility and power, only to see them become selfish and self-seeking when they reach their goals. When this happens they begin to lose followers as their egos interfere with their true skills. Usually the first skill lost to ego is the ability to listen and then the loss of personal warmth begins to alienate others. If you feel this occurring, **stop,** and then reevaluate your position before you lose creditability. You owe it to yourself and all those who respect you, to always do your best.

As you campaign for a better life, your character is a key ingredient in building it. Stay focused, make right decisions, treat others with respect and you will receive the benefits of living with a character which is formed with integrity.

"Consideration for others is the basis of a good life, a good society." **Confucius**

Chapter Six

Personal Warmth

How to make people feel at ease with you

Having people feel at ease with you, wither you know them or not, is one of life's joys many never experience. Sitting down talking with others in a casual manner, with no pressure makes you an enjoyable person. Often during these casual, relaxing conversations the true feelings for your friends emerge. It is here, when your personal warmth is displayed to others that allow them to appreciate your real love for life. Also, your true love for others will show like a beacon. I want to share two stories which touched my personal life making me appreciate others who display vast measures of personal warmth.

A certain Shrine club holds a monthly BBQ with superb food and the people are always friendly and accommodating. I go when I am able for the relaxed time spent with friends as well as the BBQ. As one of the first through the buffet, I faced the decision of where to sit. Before the buffet opened, I had just mingled without locating a table or seat. Now, with the tables empty and their occupants in line, I had no idea which seats were open. What to do? I decided to sit and begin to eat then if someone claimed the seat, I would move on, no big deal.

After I sat, a man and wife arrived to sit next to me. They admitted they were in the same situation wondering if they had taken someone's seat. Just minutes later, three ladies arrived and informed us the seats were open and they would enjoy our company. Feeling relieved, I found the food even tasted better. Names were exchanged, but I am one of those people with the problem of remembering names.

In this case, names were not important. It's what transpired during the next half hour as we six enjoyed our dinner. All the ladies were widows and that evening they touched my life. None had been to the BBQ banquet for more than five years, but at one's suggestion they decided to attend for the food and good company.

They shared memories of the good times they had here with their husbands. This event had meant a great deal to their husbands and they had enjoyed attending. But it went further than just a good time and good food. All their husbands were Shriners and this was a Shrine function. An important part of their story concerned what the Shrine meant to them after their husbands were gone. A connection, a helping hand, a friendly atmosphere abounded with a sense of security when they were in the company of Shiriners.

The story made me feel good about the Shrine, what it represents and how its members help each other. I am glad these three ladies decided to come out that night, and thankful I sat with them to hear their story of the wonderful things we enjoy. I hope to see them again as their personal warmth made me feel good for days. I'm sure they touch others lives as they did mine where ever they go.

I firmly believe in recognizing people who do outstanding work. I try to always let people know when they have done well. It gives me a great feeling to praise others, and to watch their faces glow with pride. There is something about seeing others appreciation after being recognized for their efforts. Sometimes it is as simple as a slap on the back and saying **"good job, keep up the good work."** Other times is involves a firm handshake combined with eye to eye contact and a few words of thanks. Few things are better than a personal phone call or a short note to let someone know how much you appreciate their efforts. It is a sign of personal warmth and your love of others if you let them know how proud you are of them.

One of my daughters, Lisa, played high school basketball. She was a team leader and chosen team captain in her senior year earning a basketball scholarship to college. I love sports and enjoyed that one of my children would play college ball and attended most games. In her senior year, the team earned an invitation to the NAIA Women's National Tournament. This was the first time Warner Southern ever made it to a national championship tournament. What made it sweeter for me was that Lisa was elected the team's captain. I could not have been prouder of my daughter and this hard working group of young women.

For me one of the most memorable moments in Lisa's sports career did not take place on the basketball court. It did not even occur about the year of their greatest triumphs. The moment in question happened at the school's basketball awards banquet. As I sat at the dinner, I enjoyed the love and support the girls showed each other. Touched by the personal warmth that night, I decided while driving home to recognize it in some manner. I wrote an article to the school paper. I sent a copy to each of Lisa's teammates, coaches, and the school administration. I wanted the girls to know how much I appreciated them and how they had touched my life. The following is the article:

This past week I had the opportunity to attend my daughter Lisa's end of the year Basketball Banquet. It was a nice affair with all of the girls, some of them had their boyfriends there and a few of them had their parents in attendance. Many of the girls attend college from far away and it was not possible for their parents to attend. One of the girls is even from Sweden.

A Baby Grand Piano was in the room, I mentioned it shortly after I arrived, and one of the girls told me she would play it for me later. After a nice meal and some interesting stories from the girls, it was time for the Coach to do some talking. He started out by inspiring all of the girls on the job they did over the past season. This was not a team that won a lot of games, but it was a team that, by the end of the year began to gel together. This in itself gives many of them hope for a better record next year. Something all of us need in our life is to see where

we have been, know what is possible, and to set our goals for the coming year.

The evening was wrapped up by the presentation of three special awards. These awards were determined by the girls themselves thru a secret ballot. I really did not know what to expect, even though I had attended many of the games over the past year, this team of Lisa's I never seemed to connect with. Over the past seven years that she has played ball, I knew all of the girls on a personal basis. However because of the miles I had to travel to attend these games I just never got to put the names and the faces together. I could put all of them together with a number, the one they wore during the games. Now at the banquet with all of the girls dressed up, I would look at them and see their face and try to think of what number they wore.

The coach began to announce the three best awards as selected by their teammates. First was the most improved player, this was number 32, and I fully agreed with this selection. This young lady advanced a long way from the start of the season, and what a benefit she became to the team.

Then the award for the most valuable player, who would this be? Yes, just as I would have picked it, number 23. A freshman who gave her all and that made her fun to watch. What a treat she will be for this team for the next three years.

The third award was a tough one. This was the award for the member of the team that was selected the most inspiring. The player that kept everyone up, ready to play, the one all looked to for motivation. I did not have a clue on this one, as I mentioned before I did not get to know these girls on a personal basis this year. And the winner was, as selected by her teammates, number 24. Wow, I would have never known. This beautiful young lady did not play often, in fact in many games she did not play at all. Tears came to my eyes, as I sat across from this girl and saw her beaming face. She found her place on this team, and did her best. She was being recognized by all of her peers, something some of us never get to feel. I felt so proud of her, and I really did not even know her. She had every opportunity to be disappointed, or down on herself during the year, but instead she raised everyone else on the team to a new and higher level. This is what each of us can do if in the right frame of mind, if we go out and do our best. If you do someone will recognize it, guaranteed.

As Lisa and I were getting ready to leave, one of the girls came up to me smiling. She held my hand and asked, "Are you ready for me to play the piano for you now?" I looked at her, it was the young lady who touched the whole team with her warm personal charm and motivation. Now, just as she does in her way of life, making people feel special, she was doing to me. Her focus is on people and making them feel good. Soon she played the piano for all to hear.

Who says an old man cannot go to college and learn something? I did. And it was from the Warner Southern Women's Basketball team. The lesson was to go out and make someone feel SPECIAL today!!

To this day, years after the event, I find myself emotional when I remember that evening. The occasion exemplified the personal warmth of a younger, caring generation. The young lady demonstrated this clearly by always focusing on others.

Always! It could not have been clearer that her love for life was in seeing others excel. In doing so she earned the respect and a special place in everyone's hearts.

"We make a living by what we get, but we make a life by what we give."

Winston Churchill

Chapter Seven

Charisma

The Art of Developing an Appealing and Magnetic Personality

Often we hear someone say, "He certainly has charisma. With a personality like that, he is sure to go to the top." What is meant by having charisma? **Charisma contains passion and enthusiasm that is polished.** Charisma is described as a magical ability, a certain personality characteristic with a powerful aura. Although descriptions of charisma may vary, they share the consensus that charismatic leaders inspire followers **"to**

perform above and beyond the call of duty" by appealing to emotions and enduring motives. Greatness usually accompanies charisma, as they appear hand in hand. You easily notice someone with charisma as they have a certain charm and aura about them. Certain qualities and traits of personality set them apart from average people to make them exemplary leaders. Talking with such a person naturally keeps your interest as their charm earns your respect and the interest of everyone around.

Charisma is the ability to inspire and build enthusiasm in others though use of personal charm and influence. Someone with real charisma has the power to motivate and lead combined with a personal magnetism which makes people want to be around them. Being a good listener, believing in people, and treating others the way one would want to be treated are hallmarks of a charismatic leader. They understand it can be as simple as making others feel good about what they are doing, and then making them feel appreciated.

Several years ago my daughter, Carrie, received a school assignment to talk with a grandparent about what they remembered most about one of their parents. Selecting her grandmother, Nana, Carrie explained the assignment. After a few minutes of thought, Nana answered, **"I would have to say it would be her charisma."** She continued, "I came from a family of six children. My mother motivated and inspired each of us. She showed this ability to make us always feel good about ourselves, and that we were doing our best. Somehow, and I can not imagine how she did this, but each of us six always believed that we were her favorite. She made each of us feel so special about our relationship with her that we gave her all our love and respect. She had charisma. That encouraged each of us kids to constantly improve ourselves."

Some believe having charisma is a divine gift with which we are born. You either have it or you don't. Many people I have known this seems to be the case, that God touched them leaving this gift; but I know it can be learned and earned. I believe it is developed by any individual who is serious about improving their character through mastering good people skills. **Your personality is controlled by you and you alone as an individual working to build better relationships with others.** If you have a leadership role, wither as a parent, at church, with a civic group, or at your work having any degree of charismatic personality will help achieve goals.

I have always felt my wife Anne to be very charismatic. **Her style of charisma fits in under the magnetic personality traits of being concerned about others.** She is an excellent listener and has the ability to always make others feel important in all of her conversations. Others enjoy talking with her and always seem to appreciate her company. What I love about it is that it happens so naturally for her. She makes me proud of the way she handles herself and for the example she sets for our children.

Leaders such as coaches, teachers, and parents have a large impact on how to build a charismatic nature through example. A leader by example has an effect on how their followers treat others. Working under a harsh unfeeling leader may make you more likely to be the same with your subordinates. By the same token working for a compassionate and considerate person that shows love and respect for his peers, and then the chances are you will build personal qualities in the mold of his example.

A person however exalted his position will do better work and put forth greater effort under a spirit of approval than under a cloud of criticism. You must remember that if you move in positions of leadership, you will be the one setting the tone for others. Communicating appreciation and approval to others will insure that they continue looking to you for further leadership. Remember this, sincere praise will be effective. Insincerity will make you appear manipulative. I suggest a positive charismatic personality will take you to a higher level of success.

I Suggest a Positive Charismatic Personality Will Take You to a Higher Level of Success

Charisma grows as you become more confident. It shows in your positive body language. How you handle yourself and treat others is a key component as to how others view your personality. You may ask, "Where do I start?" It can be as simple as believing in others, and then letting them know you believe in them. Make everyone feel needed and important. Another indication of your growing charisma to followers is being positive, enthusiastic, and concerned about their welfare. Charisma should be a natural, visionary way of life where you begin building a fascinating, captivating and charming lifestyle.

Chapter Eight

Possessing a Proven Record

The Portrait of a Leader is Painted By his Record of Accomplishments

"We are what we repeatedly do." **Aristotle**

A proven history of past accomplishments is critical to how others view your qualification to further leadership opportunities. The fact you have been tried and tested and emerged successful will demonstrate that you are qualified to lead. Many of the challenges we pursue in life are met by providing your past record. Whether applying for a job, or a loan, entrance into university, or running for political office, your record is the statement of ability. Possessing a proven record of accomplishments will set your stature. A clean past will open many doors, whereas a shameful, mysterious, or questionable past will complicate future options.

People talk about the methods to find a good leader. "How can we find a qualified person as a replacement for this position?" "Where do we look, and then how do we know if he is qualified." The answer is checking his record and achievements.

Leaders, Where Do They Come From?

Leaders, where do they come from? How would you describe a good leader? I am certain if I were to ask everyone what describes a good leader; I would receive a multitude of different answers. Some might say a good leader is one who motivates, someone to really get you going. Another might answer, a good leader is someone who dots all the I's and crosses all the T's. Still another could believe a good leader is someone who is a good people person, one that communicates.

The one I believe fits best and sums up what makes a good leader. "A good leader is someone that takes you to a place that you would not normally go by yourself." I love that quote, let me repeat it. "A good leader is someone that takes you to a place that you would not normally go by yourself".

The next question should be, how does the good leader do this? It has been said, a good leader has the ability to

76

stimulate you. So, a good leader has the ability to "**stimulate you to go to a place you would not normally go by yourself.**" I'm sure each of you has someone like this in your life. Surely, you had a teacher, or a coach, or a friend that had the ability to get you excited enough that you would do more than you thought you could. This person brought out the best in you, and would stimulate you.

A synonym for the word, stimulate, is aggravate. So, it could be inferred that a good leader is one who "**aggravates you to go to a place you would not normally go by yourself.**" I love this one too. I am sure you have had someone in your life like this. He could have been an employer who at times became aggravating, but when all was said and done, you accomplished more than you expected because of his constant aggravation. He may have been annoying; but he pushed you to more production.

Another word for aggravate is irritate. This works too, but if you are married, I suggest you not try this on your spouse. If you irritate your spouse to much, no one is happy. It could be said then a leader has the ability to, "**irritate you to go to a place you would not normally go by yourself.**" In the past my children have told me that I am the most irritating person in the world, simply because I expect them to do their homework, keep their rooms clean, and to do their chores. And yet, through my irritating them, they became better people, they learned responsibility, and may become good future leaders.

I use a story of cod fish in my talks about leaders and where they come from. It usually garners a few chuckles, but it makes you think about qualities that help a leader or organization to succeed. As you read, think about how its principals could be used to your benefit.

For a long time, I thought of cod fish being the little four inch square fish cake inside the MacDonald's bun. Actually the cod is one of the major commercial fish. Caught in the hundreds of millions on the Atlantic shelf along the Newfoundland Banks, they account for a major portion of the northeast commercial fishing industry.

Some years past, a group of business men formed a company to catch, clean, package, and freeze them for shipment all across the United States. As with all new businesses there appeared to be a glitch, frozen cod did not taste the same and didn't have the white flaky texture.

When you have a problem in business, you find a solution. The men had the great idea of building large tank cars, filling them with salt water and cod, and then shipping them across the country alive. Wrong solution, the cod still tasted different and the texture was the same as frozen. It seems the cod were becoming lazy and lethargic in their fancy water filled tank cars. Their muscles began to deteriorate.

Same problem, new solution. Some smart man considered the need to make the cod exercise during their train ride. How do you convince a cod fish of the necessity to exercise so he will be tasty and have nice flaky white meat? This smart man knew that the catfish is the natural enemy of the cod, so into each of the tank cars they would sprinkle a few catfish to accompany the cod across this great nation. The catfish chased the cod up, down, and all around the tank cars, so when the cod arrived on someone's dinner table, they were in the best shape of their lives. **The catfish stimulated, aggravated, and irritated the cod all the way to their destination.**

I challenge each of you to be the catfish in your organization. As leaders, go out to stimulate, aggravate, and irritate everyone to be the best, the very best they can be.

Part of a leader's proven record is based on how willing he is to work to find success no matter how much time it takes. A quote by Andrew Carnegie that I like, says so much about character and an individual's willingness to succeed. **"The average person puts in only 25% of his energy and ability into his work. The world takes off its hat to those who put in more than 50% of their capacity, and stands on its head for those few and far between souls who devote 100%. As I grow older, I pay less attention to what men say, I just watch what they do."** It is so true; you learn volumes about someone simply by watching how they work with others.

Be a Proven Leader!

"Failure is only the opportunity to more intelligently begin again."

Henry Ford

Chapter Nine

Thinking Outside the Box

An Open Mind and the Ability to Seek Unknown Solutions is a Talent Worth Developing

The cliché **"Thinking outside the box"** is a term used as an invitation to be creative and imaginative in your thinking. According to Albert Einstein, **"Problems cannot be solved by thinking within the framework in which they were created."** Few people possess the ability to get serious and come up with creative and original ideas. I find people who are creative out of the box thinkers have an ability to lead others to think out of the box. Creative thinking needs an open mind and a willingness to see the world from a different or unusual perspective. They explore and nurture new ways to perform tasks and know you must act to make them reality.

An open mind filled with ideas will be able to accept new solutions to future programs and the wisdom to implement them. Having these abilities will test the depths of your thinking when looking for a problem's solution. It means viewing the task from every direction, and then turning it inside out and upside down to search for the best answer. People, who think outside the box, have no limits on their vision as they advance towards a workable solution.

"Thinking outside the box" requires one to go against the normal ways to be innovative and break common thought patterns. These thinkers are ready to go against the grain and be inventive enough to look at problems from a different prospective. Innovative thinkers have the extraordinary talent to go beyond brainstorming to become a creative thinker. They have the resilience and spirit to accept scorn and ridicule from those who cannot or will not see a task from a different viewpoint.

Sometime their ideas seem off the wall, but within one idea rest the kernel for another one that will be right on target. After generating ideas, the time comes to decide which warrant action and which have the potential for further study. Looking at every possible way for improvement stretches the minds of all on the team. By asking "what if", the out of the box thinker draw others to consider different directions and sometimes find new solutions or improvements to old ideas. Accepting the impossible is valid only for those timid souls without the urge to go beyond the presently accepted frontiers.

You might have difficulty thinking of an "out of the box" idea that changed your life because many are common everyday. I won't even mention airplanes or other inventions which took place before most of us were born, but I will refer to Mr. Bell's telephone. Mr. Alexander Graham Bell spoke the words, ***"Mr. Watson, come here, I want you."*** Mr. Watson, Bell's associate, in another room heard those words spoken over the first primitive telephone. By the 1930's the spoken word could travel along wires from America to Europe or Asia. A good invention, so is it time to quit? After Mr. Bell., several generations of out of the box thinkers sought to conquer the impossible. Because of these men and women, you have satellite television, computers, cellular phones, and a thousand other inventions who trace parts of their ancestry to the first telephone. All this happened because some men and women would not accept the idea of impossible.

You have now decided you want to become one of these creative "out of the box" thinkers and break out of whatever box has you trapped. First, you must be willing to open your mind to the idea of exploring the unknown in an effort to find new solutions. There is no second or third, just the first. Below are suggestions to aid your creative thinking.

10 Steps to
"Thinking Outside the Box"

1. Be willing to accept and look at all possibilities regardless of how silly or impossible they might seem. Be willing to brainstorm.

2. Know exactly what is in the box now, in other words, how things are currently done. You have to know the "now", so you can compare results to see the improvement.

3. Examine how things are done, what could be left out to be more effective, what could be added to make it more precise. What must to be kept?

4. Be willing to throw out everything you are doing, and then with an open mind to start again from a new direction.

5. Approach a task by considering what you would do if there were no rules, or if there was no budget. After accumulating ideas, then figure how you can bring your new ideas inline with the rules and budget. This can be a fun challenge that will bring you amazing ideas.

6. Focus on how you can improve the situation by addressing the task from different directions. Be willing to listen to and use other's ideas.

7. Look for value, new solutions, better communications, more visibility, and economy. Then make your assumptions and work them towards your goals.

8. Be open minded enough to share your thoughts and respectful enough to listen to others thoughts as together more possibilities often appear.

9. Never, never become discouraged, regardless of how difficult the task may look. Many solutions are discovered at the last moment, or after others have given up.

10. Stay focused, you are looking for a solution or new idea that is usable and workable during extraordinary and challenging times. Your ultimate goal is to create something that you will see in use in the near future.

It takes a special person powered by commitment and curiosity to work at **"thinking outside the box"**. Great leaders are inclined to think "outside the box" for success, but you don't have to be a leader to think "outside the box". You only need a mind which allows you to do so, and the means to bring your dream to reality. In 1899, the Commissioner of the United States Patent office, Charles H. Duell announced, **"Everything that can be invented has now been invented"**. If he were here today, I wonder what he would say. Try to envision what the state of invention will be in a 100 years from today.

I am a member of a team who find methods to increase Shrine membership. Increasing a fraternal organizations membership is a challenge in today's world. Competition for an individual's time is at an all time high. Everyone is so busy it is difficult to convince them to commit to a club or organization unless you have an excellent benefit package to offer. As a committee, we are always trying to **"think outside the box"** for ideas to make the Shrine attractive to potential new members.

Recently, I sent an email to other members of the committee asking for a wish list. I asked for each to send me 5 wishes they believed would help increase membership. I specifically asked they "think outside the box" for this exercise these were wishes they would like to happen within five years. Additionally they were informed that manpower and money would be unlimited; and to let their minds run wild. I thought once we got the ideas then we would work to see if we could actually find a way to squeeze them into the budget and make them happen.

The response was outstanding because they did reach way "outside the box" and opened new thought processes as how we look at certain areas. It is simple to get people thinking in new and different directions and to brainstorm for new solutions by removing the restraints of money and manpower. Certain members of the group would be hesitant to offer solutions during round table discussions, but would attack the problems aggressively and with more thought by email. I attribute this to answering questions while alone with no one around to input any negative feelings to their answer. Their answers were pure and given without any restrictions on their thought process to reach a much needed solution for a major challenge.

"There are No Rules Here – We're Trying to Accomplish Something"

Successfully gathering the ideas made me think of a quote by Thomas Edison, **"There are no rules here-----**

we're trying to accomplish something. I never did anything by accident, nor did any of my invention come by accident; they came by work." Edison, one of the greatest inventors of all time with 1093 United States patents, a man who must have constantly lived outside the box. You have the tools to think "outside the box", you only need the desire and commitment to start. Open your mind and dream.

"We are all travelers in the wilderness of this world, and the best we can find in our travels is an honest friend."

Robert Louis Stevenson

Chapter Ten

Working on Your People Skills

Success is not the Results of One Man's Thoughts or Activities, but Lies in the Help of Others

A smartly dressed middle aged couple holding hands enter the room on a Saturday evening. A casual atmosphere fills the room with groups chatting, and a small band playing lively music for the several couples on the dance floor. This handsome couple greets everyone with a handshake or hug as they wander about the room. Some people are friends, others they meet for the first time. Either way, their people skills are evident as their friends anxiously wait to greet them.

A friendly aura precedes them as they offer a friendly smile to every person. They clearly understand the importance of effective communication shown in their ability to begin a conversation with anyone. It was evident their popularity and acceptance they received rested on their ability to make each person they spoke to feel good about themselves. You understood that this couple finds joy in making a difference in others lives.

Recently, a dear friend of my wife and I passed away. Sometime later, we saw her gentleman friend. The two of them in their 70's found a new life together after their spouses passed away. During our talk, he shared a memory that made us feel good. He said, "She loved both of you so much, you both made her feel so good. Often, we would be at a function and she would lean over to me and say, Gary and Anne are here." Later, she had said, "When ever Gary and Anne were in the room, and it does not matter how many people are present, I know, that sometime before the night is over they will be by to give me a hug and say hello." It brought tears to think our actions were so appreciated and meant so much to someone. It was a testimony to the results good people skills will achieve.

Possessing good people skills can be worth their weight in gold. In today's world, the competition for positions, jobs, or assignments often depend on your abilities to work with people. This skill may swing the pendulum just enough to give you the advantage. It becomes increasingly important as you move up the leadership ladder to fine tune your people skills. Two or more people often compete for the same job, each with similar technical ability. The final decision of who gets the promotion or assignment usually rest on who has the better communication skills.

Good people skills are evident in your confidence and belief in what you are doing. Charisma is reflected in your personal warmth. It also means you care about others and are willing to listen to their needs. Combined together it means you have the ability to converse meaningfully with anybody and develop good relationships. I believe the happiness in life is directly tied to the quality and number of close relationships you initiate. If there is any one main component of being a people person it is found in the quality of being a good communicator. Those of you that are comfortable expressing yourself to your friends will have a long life of happiness. As you grow older, you will reap the rewards of having many friends who love and respect you.

Below are characteristics that should be developed to build exceptional people skills. Those who master and practice them as a normal part of life will be rewarded.

Resolves disputes
Builds relationships
An excellent listener
Humble and gracious
Easy to converse with
Warm and considerate
Finds the best in others
Always supportive to others
Makes a positive impression
Honest, loyal and respectful

Work on these ten points to build your people skills and you will soon see positive results. The benefit of being a **"skilled people person"** is in understanding how to react with others under varied situations. When you master these skills you will dramatically increase the positive way people respond to you.

President Ronald Reagan known as the **Great Communicator** possessed some of the best people skill I have ever seen. Although I never personally met him, I studied him and other Presidents of the United States. President Reagan radiated a personal allure which others enjoyed and wanted to be a part of. Quick with his wit and entertaining with his stories, he kept people smiling and entertained. If one looked into the meanings of his entertaining stories, you find deep philosophical beliefs that were the hallmarks of this great man.

In books I have read about him, I learned more about his people skills. Even as the most powerful man in the world, others regarded him to be a modest man. How he saw his place on this earth is illustrated in this quote. "**Whatever else history may say about me when I am gone, I hope it will record that I appealed to your best hopes, not your worst fears, to your confidence rather than your doubts. My dream is that you will travel the road ahead with liberty's lamp guiding your steps and opportunity's arm steadying your way.**"

Regardless of your position in life, as a bag boy at the supermarket, or as President of the United States, people skills remain important to success. Look at ways to improve your people skills to use them in your **Campaign for a Better Life.** Write down how you would like to improve and refer to it often to make you more conscious of your goals. If you sincerely work at it, the results will come quickly and you will be richly rewarded.

"What's important is that one strives to achieve a goal"

Ronald Reagan

Chapter Eleven

Motivational Skills

Working to Help Others Find the Best Within Themselves

I remember being motivated by my third grade teacher, Mrs. Dummer. I was only one of many who she inspired to become better students. She stimulated her students by her attitude and beliefs that you could do better if you would just try. As a single woman in her sixties who bought a new 1963 black on black Corvette, she became the idol of every boy in school. We would watch her wheel into the school parking lot grey hair blowing in the wind. She allowed our young minds to discover our true potential and see the person we truly wanted to be. Possessing the quality to stimulate, she persuaded us to be our very best. **She was a quiet effective motivator** of young people by allowing them to believe in themselves.

A few years later, I met another motivator in my life. My high school football coach came charging into my life. He made tremendous physical demands of my flabby body and stressed my brain to learn football plays. All the physical and mental challenges were secondary to his primary objective to make us a team. He was highly motivated to take this bunch of **wanna be** football players and mold them into a unit. He began by instilling fear by telling us that half would fall by the wayside within three weeks. Twice a day practices, the first at 6:30 a.m. took a toll on our numbers. Wind sprints in 100 degree temperature made your body scream. Blocking, tackling, everything was a test of desire and motivation. It was the method of separating the **wanna be's** from the players. The coach's sole motivation was to field **a team.**

This form of motivation is one I had never encountered before. I did not like any part of it. In fact, I did not consider it to be motivating at that time. To me the whole program seemed over done, cruel, and merciless. On some afternoons following practice, my body suggested vehemently that it not return for the morning practice.

A realization came over me when in my new uniform at the pep rally. I now knew the sweat and sore muscles were worth the effort. **We became a team through the motivation of a coach who cared about us as individuals.** He made us understand that no one of us could win the game alone. The star quarterback depended on the offensive line to protect him, as the running back needed the blockers to open the lane for him to run. The defense's job simply put was to stop the other team. For many of us, this was the first time we had to depend on someone doing their job, so we could be successful at our own job.

The team's goal was to win the game on Friday night. Winning was good, but it became clear the friendships and the lessons of teamwork were just as valuable. Today, I can not tell you the scores of any of those games, but I remember the motivating lesson taught by playing them. President Harry S. Truman summed it up saying, **"It is amazing what you can accomplish if you do not care who gets the credit."**

It Is Amazing What You Can Accomplish If You Do Not Care Who Gets the Credit

Over the years I, as most have, worked for an individual who motivated your life. Often a boss becomes not only your leader, but a friend, an inspiration, and a mentor. Perhaps the single most important basic skill in motivating others lays in treating people the same as you wish to be treated, as a responsible professional. Many never develop this skill that needs a balance of respect, dignity, fairness, incentives, and guidance. Develop that skill and you will motivate others to be more effective. Success in learning the proper methods to motivate, will find others more willing to listen and be more receptive in accepting your leadership.

Motivation is a two way street. The most inspirational people who I have worked for or with have been **the ones who believed in me.** They motivated me not only by challenging me, but by allowing me to express myself. They released the reins to let me do the job. Oh, I am certain they kept watch over me from a distance. Delegating responsibility can be a powerful form of motivation. When people understand you trust them to do great things, they will work hard to live up to those expected standards and justify your faith. People feel motivated when they know they make a contribution or difference. Complements and credit given for good work continues to motivate the person to increase their abilities and to develop additional skills.

In recent years working as a leader in the volunteer organization of the Shriners has been both fun and rewarding especially in support of the Shriners Hospitals for Children. Motivating others has taken on a new look or purpose in this setting. It becomes more important to appeal to other's sense of pride, to their love of friendships, and their need to help others; especially the children who can not help themselves. The motivation comes from feeling respect, in compliments, in recognition, and the knowledge they really make a difference in the lives of others. The sum of all these parts is the sense of fulfillment you receive. It isn't about money or a bigger office. **It's about a pat on the back for a job well done and the sincere thank you that motivates people who love volunteer groups.**

Shriners love fun and many of them live for the competition. I have seen men so motivated to get the best score in a clown competition, or the fastest time on a motorcycle obstacle course, and for what? The prize is a small trophy. But, along with the trophy come the bragging rights and the knowledge that you did your best, and your best was good enough to gain you first place. People need that extra little something in their life, however small. We all have a desire to feed our self worth and esteem so that tomorrow we will wake up with added enthusiasm and confidence. Motivation is the fuel that keeps the human engine running. Motivation comes from within; this in turn helps to build character. I found one of the best ways to keep others motivated was to create an environment where every person feels valuable and important. This is especially true in a volunteer organization.

In sharing these short motivational stories with you, it should be clear that the "**how to**" motivate others varies from situation to situation. A person, who is a real motivator, spends time studying each circumstance to get the best effective type of stimulation in place for the job at hand. There are people who are experts at motivating others with stimulating inspiration; they have a bag full of tools to which they turn. A positive personality along with a determined demeanor is what keeps the motivated person on top of their game.

Following are a few characteristics of methods used to stimulate and motivate others, thereby giving them a reason to act. You would use different methods for different applications of getting others to reach their full potential. The next time you look for ways to motivate others consider this list, and then build your plan of motivation:

Challenges
Appreciation, Pride
Emotional, Heartfelt
For a Positive Purpose
Reason to Act, Urgency
Charitable, Contributions
Monetary, Security, Trust
Enthusiastic, Encouraging

By Example, Be a Listener
Benefit to Others, Influence
Spiritual, Making a Difference
Opportunity, Delegate Decisions
Reason or Incentive, Recognition
Appeal to Their Needs, Build Confidence
Social Status, Feeling of Accomplishment
Expecting the Best, Developing Advancement

As you develop motivational skills, it is important to understand people's needs. **Motivation is the art of getting people to do what you want because they want to do it.** Often their needs, desires, or "hot buttons" will be divulged through your listening. As soon as you know 'the button' to turn them on, or what motivates them, your job becomes simple. Being a good listener brings numerous benefits. Relationships will improve, performance is enhanced, team spirit grows, morale increases, and enthusiasm with rise. Good listening skills also bring with it trust. When all these characteristics align motivation will peak.

You have to earn trust through excellent communications. Work openly and encourage others to brainstorm along with you as you build and motivate. Remember positive motivation becomes very contagious. Every person you involve in the planning and implementation will also become a supporter. Keep in mind that motivation is one of those catchall words that have different meanings to different people. Through the practice of listening for others needs, and then by giving them reason to act, you will find yourself being seen as a motivator.

Being an enthusiastic motivational leader can be a challenge, it demands a resolute dedicated commitment towards inspiring others. Workers in today's business world will not accept or listen to dictatorial leaders who try to rule with an iron hand and a loud voice. It is not an acceptable way of doing business and certainly will not motivate anyone. Motivators, today, must perform many functions as friend, coach, mentor, leader, and confidante. **True motivators work at it every day, not just when they feel the need.**

Standards for identifying leaders change. No longer is a leader judged simply by his experience, training, or expertise. How a person behaves becomes important along with their motivational skills and how effectively they relate to their people. Lee Iacocca, former CEO of Chrysler Corporation, once said, **"Management is nothing more than motivating other people."** People who are unable to motivate themselves will have to be happy with mediocrity regardless of their talent and qualifications because it would be impossible for them to motivate others. However, we know you can succeed at most any task for which you have unlimited enthusiasm.

> *"A hundred times a day I remind myself that my life depends on the labors of other men, living and dead, and that I must exert myself in order to give, in the measure as I have received, and am still receiving. Try not to become a man of success but rather try to become a man of value."* **Albert Einstein**

Over the years, I have focused on motivating others whither it was trying to get Jason, my son, to take his first step or another son, Jared, to pass his driving test. My test in life has been attempting to get my employees to improve their quality of work, or to get hundreds of Shriners to volunteer time for charity. I consider my ability to arouse enthusiasm in men and women my greatest asset. One way to develop a person's best effort is by showing appreciation and providing encouragement.

What means most and makes me feel best is understanding that I may have had some small part in others achieving more than they thought possible. Seeing the smiles and the sense of accomplishment in others after they have been motivated to exceed their own expectations fills my being with exhilaration.

Every person has the desire to be recognized as a valuable human being. Sometimes they just need a little motivation to get there. You could be the answer to their prayers. Practices your motivational skills as you "**campaign for a better life**", the rewards are tremendous.

Chapter Twelve

Becoming a Great Communicator

Effective Communication is the Most Important Quality in Building Leaders

"The most important single ingredient in the formula of success is knowing how to get along with people" **Theodore Roosevelt**

Effective communication has to be one of the toughest jobs in today's world. The world around us is modernizing in the communication fields faster than we can imagine. The electronic technology surpasses the dreams of men of just two decades ago. With cell phones and email available to the masses, I still prefer to sit down face to face with someone. There is still nothing better than looking someone in the eye as you exchange information.

A good communicator must be familiar with all communication methods. A speaker must be blessed with certain eloquence; but also possess a command of non-verbal techniques. Recent research states that **up to 70% of all communication today is non-verbal.** This is amazing, but it reinforces the need for a positive body attitude. As a communicator your presence and actions will be on display. Studies show any contradiction between a speaker's actions and words, the audience will read the actions as the truth. It is important to be sure your physical behavior does not get in the way of you verbal message.

Good written and electronic media skills are a requirement in disseminating information in the fast paced community today. You must be able to listen, not just hear, at levels in your contact with people. Understanding your personal contact has varied components of personal information, business data, dreams, and ambitions, you gain the keys to communication. The ability to remember small items of personal information such as hobbies, birthdays, special interest or upcoming events will help convey interest and open the way to bi-lateral communication. Good communication is a gift to you and to others.

A good communicator learns the rules of etiquette and personal conduct of the group or society he is entering and diligently practices them. A professional demeanor combined with a clear and accurate delivery will let his audience see him as an able communicator. You receive the greatest compliment when you are asked for your opinion. It shows they care about and respect your thoughts enough to hear them.

Communication is multi-lateral and must be treated as such to be effective. Most people think only of the verbal side of communication. The verbal is only the foundation; it takes many more elements to be effective. The following are ten key elements to build good communications:

Stay Positive
Be Prepared
Use Visual Aids
Listen to Feedback
Use a Good Delivery
Be Consistent and Honest
Use Your Nonverbal Skills
Use Emotions and Be Sincere
Be Sure You Are Understood
Leave a Lasting Impression

Confucius may have said it best hundreds of years ago when he said, **"Tell me and I'll forget, Show me and I'll remember, Involve me and I'll understand."**

We can develop the best laid plans in concert with the most qualified leaders of our time; but if we fail to communicate effectively, by today's standards, our dreams and plans will prove to be nothing more than loose sand in a high wind.

I want to share some history about communications. My purpose is to show how fast communication is changing. My hope is you will feel an increased urgency in your life. Mass communication began in 1440 with Johannes Gutenberg, a German inventor. His invention of a printing press which remained with modification and increased mechanization the principal means of printing into the late 20th century until the advent of computer printing techniques. In the first 60 years of mechanical printing an estimated 15 million books had been pressed, representing thirty thousand titles.

Basic knowledge or information doubled in about 100 year increments from the 16th through the 19th centuries. We entered the 20th century using the same Gutenberg lead type to print words on paper, but exited it with the computer language of teraflops. In the 1950's and 60s, computers startled the world with the word kilobyte. This meant information could be crunched by a machine calculating at a 1000 functions per second (2 to the 10th power). Kilo gave way to megabytes, gigabytes to today when we speak of teraflops, a trillion operations per second (2 to the 40th power). IBM in collaboration with the Department of Energy's NNSA/ Lawrence Livermore Laboratory built the Blue Gene/L computer with a peak speed of 360 teraflops. Scientists are already working on a computer that will function in the realm of a petaflop, quadrillion functions per second.

Some smart person with time on his hands figured if you took all the knowledge/information available on the world wide web and printed it Gutenberg style in books of 500 pages, and then stacked the books one on top another that the stack would reach beyond the moon. A more startling fact is that same information reduced by computer to magnetic disc could be housed in a small room. The knowledge/information is doubling every 60 days.

Granted the vast majority of this explosion of knowledge/information falls in the scientific fields such as medicine, astronomy, etc., that still leaves huge quantities that impact on your daily lives. My question now is how much have your communication skills improved? Are you keeping up with the times, staying even, or are you falling behind? **Communication is changing at every level, are you?**

Over the years, I have accumulated a series of communication points and axioms that I use in my speaking engagements. I enjoy making presentations, speaking, and improving my ability to communicate. Always seeking ways to improve myself, I listen to other speakers and read to improve my non-verbal skills. Every time I hear, read, or witness something I believe will help me I write it down. Below are 20 key points I personally use in preparation for a speaking engagement.

20 Tips to Improve Your Communication Skills When Presenting Yourself to One or One Hundred

1. Your message should teach people and organizations methods to surpass themselves.

2. Your goal as a good communicator should be to improve your skills to the point they become natural and effortless.

3. Good communication skills include use of a likeable personality and positive body language.

4. The use of negative or profane language degrades you and your message.

5. A good communicator is knowledgeable and prepared when making a presentation. Do not use information that has not been researched, it can work against you.

6. The most important aspect of communicating is being a good listener.

7. Nervousness and anxiety will be overcome with good preparation.

8. Practice of your communication skills brings confidence and ability.

9. Good communicators mix humor and stories with the facts of the presentation.

10. When you make a presentation to a group, how you dress is an important part of your first impression.

11. Most audiences form their impression of you in the first three minutes. Plan a good opening.

12. Being a good communicator is not about perfection, it's about achieving objectives and communicating your message. Successful communication is determined how others interpret it.

13. Your awareness of how you are being received, and the ability to adjust the presentation to the needs of the audience will enable you to keep their attention.

14. Be able to tell stories with meaning, they can inspire and help to get your message out.

15. You can have the right idea, the best intentions, talent; but if you do not communicate well, the message will be lost.

16. When making a presentation, stay within the allotted time frame. Your effectiveness diminishes substantially when you run over time.

17. Using visuals in your presentation will double the amount of information others retain. The use of charts, graphs, or Power Point is an excellent addition to gain added effect.

18. Communication requires you to fully understand what you are presenting if you expect to be understood.

19. Giving Praise during communication will let others know you appreciate them and will create a more constructive atmosphere.

20. The final impression you make on the audience is the one they will remember, make it good.

Gary Bergenske

Gary Bergenske

What Distinguishes Winners is their Will to Prepare to Win.

Repetition can be good if you have a point that you want to be sure is received by your audience. An old saying reinforces this, "First you tell 'em what you are going to tell 'em, then you tell 'em, then you tell 'em what you told 'em!"

The importance of good communication skills is exemplified in a survey of recruiters from companies with more than 5,000 employees. Communication skills were cited as the single most important decisive factor in choosing managers. The survey, conducted by the University of Pittsburgh's Katz Business School, points out that communication skills, including written and oral presentations, as well as an ability to work with others, are the main factors contributing to job success and advancement.

The ability to communicate ideas with others is one of the most powerful tools of a great leader. The art of bringing information to life leaves a lasting impression. To close this chapter, I want to share a great quote from President Ronald Reagan's farewell address on January 11, 1989: **"I won the nickname, *The Great Communicator*. But I never thought it was my style or the words I used that made a difference. It was the content. I wasn't a great communicator, but I communicated great things, and they didn't spring full bloom from my brow, they came for the heart of a great nation--- from our experience, our wisdom, and our belief in the principals that have guided us for two centuries. They called it the Reagan revolution. Well, I'll accept that, but for me it always seemed more like the great rediscovery, a rediscovery of our values and our common sense."**

Chapter Thirteen

Let Your Passions Shine Through

Desire and Commitment Will Put Your Passions to Work and Change Your Life

"I never did a day's work in my life. It was all fun." **Thomas A. Edison**

T he intense enthusiasm some individuals have for life, or a particular activity separates them from the crowd. It is a combination of their emotional state to be true to themselves; and the ability to give a total effort. People of this breed always perform at their best. Because they care so much about success, time and effort become secondary. The time clock doesn't govern their work, only the completion of the task matters. What concerns them most are the love, desire, and enjoyment of what they do. Use your passion to move projects forward, help nurture relationships, and therefore rise to a higher level. I am talking about working with passion. Find your passion, whatever it might be, and then work with it in all you do and it will become a trait of your character.

> ### *The highest degree of commitment comes with passion attached to it.*

Great athletes, leaders, coaches, and teachers understand the need for passion. Greatness requires commitment beyond the norm; it requires you to immersion to passion. Passion means you possess the strong desire, the intense emotions and the unlimited enthusiasm to drive you to finding solutions. There is no such thing as playing the game with partial passion, either you are or you are not passionate about it. **Where you find strong passion, you will find success close by.** Passionate people emit so much positive energy they are a joy to be around. We learn from watching passionate people. Their passion is contagious.

I would like to share with you a story about passion in our youth. It's a true story about my daughter Carrie. We moved to the Orlando area when she was just 7 years old and in the 2nd grade. It was a difficult for her as she had to start all over to make some new friends. It did not take long though, soon she had several new friends, but one in particular was special, she was to become a friend for life. The two of them shared many of the same passions and that helped their friendship to grow. We got to know this little girl real good as the two of them would take turns spending the night at each others home. They looked vary much alike; you would almost swear they were sisters. They were beautiful. I believe they were the two most beautiful girls in the class.

As time went on the girls friendship grew, it was into middle school and they were almost inseparable, always spending time together. By the time they began high school the friendship continued. They were both doing quite a bit of modeling, and there was a bit of competition between them. Who would get the best modeling jobs, or make the most money. It was competition, but it was friendly, each of them so proud of what the other was capable of doing. They loved and respected each other, and always tried to help the other one do her best. This I found to be a lesson from our youth, for it was always about doing your best, no matter what it was. Each of them could always count on the others support.

By the time they were seniors in high school their friendship was to be tested to the max. These two beautiful girls were the final two left in the race to be crowned as the Homecoming Queen. I can remember it as if it were just yesterday. Each of them dressed in an elegant formal long gown, with their hair up, and they looked just right. All eyes were upon them as it came close to half time of the game. It was during half time that the winner would be announced. I believe all eyes were not on them just because of their beauty, but also everyone knew what great friends they were. Everyone was looking at them to see just how their friendship would handle one of them losing. Their passion to see each other succeed was to be tested.

The two had already figured it out, they knew exactly what they were going to do. Their friendship was deep, and competition was in their blood, but they both knew how to handle it. You see one of them was going to be the Homecoming Queen, and the other one, well; she was going to be the best friend of the Homecoming Queen. This is a lesson to all of us, to do the best you can, and always be ready to support each other in the best that they do, no matter what it might be. Be happy for each other, congratulate each other, and help them to do their best. Carrie was crowned Queen and her friend could not have been more gracious or supportive. I was proud of both of them as **I knew they were setting an example to others by the way they handled themselves.**

Soon, they were out of high school and on their way to college. This time they would have many miles between them, but the friendship and passion in their lives would still continue. My daughter went to the University of South Florida in Tampa and her friend went to school in the western part of the United States. They would talk to each other on the phone regularly, and see each other when home for the holidays.

My daughter would come home from USF often for the weekend and then drive back to Tampa on Sunday afternoon. I remember this one particular Sunday afternoon perfectly, Carrie had just left to go back to school when the phone rang. The call was for my daughter, it was her best friend's sister. I told her Carrie had just left, and she asked for me to get a hold of her as soon as I could. You see, her best friend had collapsed that morning, and died of a heart attack at the age of 23.

What happened over the next few days astonished me, how these young people handled this. The way that they did it was another lesson exhibited by our youth. As expected there would be a large number of people for this funeral. You see, she was loved by everyone, so a large church was selected. Her friends decorated the halls and rooms of this church like you would not believe. There were pictures, and memento's and items of hers displayed. What a tribute to her and to the life she lived so passionately. When the time came the church quickly filled up, and a large moveable wall had to be opened to make room for more. There were several hundred people there.

A time during the service arrived, when the minister asked if anyone would like to say a few words. He asked they come forward. I've seen this done in the past, and no one ever comes forward at services I've gone to for older people. But that was not the case with this young group. They had a passion to be a part of this, to make a lasting statement about their friend. A line quickly formed, and for the next hour we listened to many stories about this young lady. There were tears, and smiles, and even a few laughs as they celebrated her life. What a lesson I learned from our youth that day.

As I look around at all of the people I know, and think of how a little more passion in their lives would help them, it excites me. Passion lies in all of us; we just need to activate it. A strong passion will ensure a better life for you. It will bring with it additional success. It does not matter where you get involved, it is only important that you get involved. Benjamin Franklin once said, "If passion drives you, let reason hold the reins." It is important to never underestimate the power of passion.

If passion drives you, let reason hold the reins."

I think of passion as the **special prize inside you.** If you find the prize inside, then work, commitment, and pleasure will all come together. You will be passionate about what you do and nothing will look impossible. To have passion is to have a dream with a mission to succeed attached to it. People who are passionate about something work and perform in the mode for success. They are totally focused on their mission to achieve significant progress.

I am certain everyone has been passionate about something in their lives. If you are truly passionate about something, you loose track of time and wonder where it went. This happens because you are enjoying what you are doing. This is when you begin to realize the power of passion. Now, what you must do it find passion in all you do. Passion develops from a great desire motivated by persistence. Passionate people achieve more and enjoy their success to a greater extent. Find ways to put more passion in what you do. You will be happier and life will be more enjoyable. When you enjoy life, you will become a person, others will enjoy. Make passion a must in your life.

Chapter Fourteen

Persistence
and
Determination

Nothing Can Take the Place of Persistence
And Determination in the Search for Success

"Never, never, never, never give up."
Winston Churchill

For about twenty years, our family has owned a condo on Daytona beach. From the balcony, we watch the varied people who populate the beach. It is enjoyable to watch the different kinds of people and see some of their crazy adventures.

One day while sitting on the balcony, I noticed two ladies, one very elderly, who seemed to be in trouble. The younger kept rubbing the older lady's hand till the older lady sat down in the sand. I felt something had to be wrong, so I took a pair of beach chairs and two bottles of cold water down to the beach to see if I could be of help.

The Unexpected Lessons That Happen in Life Are Often The Ones You Remember Most.

When I arrived, the two ladies were sitting and seemed to be okay. I explained I had been watching and became worried they might be in trouble. The younger woman's explanation could not have been more unexpected, but it made a change in how I would view life for the rest of my days.

The older lady was deaf and blind and her daughter communicated by drawing letters in the palm of her hand. She could speak, but she demonstrated the technique to me by drawing block letters in my hand. **"Thank you, for caring."** Each letter drawn precisely, so I would understand. She seemed to write in a quick script for her mother. Years of practice made the communication easier. The two were on a stroll to the pier about a quarter mile further down the beach, when the elder lady became fatigued and sat down. The mother was tired, but unwilling to cut the walk short. She just needed a short rest. They performed the walk daily during their vacation. The goal was clear, to walk to the pier and back. Unable to see or hear, the mother's other senses were keen. She enjoyed the feel of the sea breeze and the taste of the ocean spray. She loved the feel of the sand between her toes and the sensation of the warm ocean water swirling about her feet.

After a short rest, the mother indicated it was time to continue the journey. A journey that would seem trivial to most; but I found a determination in these two frail elderly women that seemed as if it could move mountains. In those few minutes, they taught me to look at the good in life no matter how bad things might seem. Despite the physical hardships, they had set a goal and were unwilling to compromise. The persistence and determination of these two women changed my attitude toward life.

I left the chairs for their return walk and returned to the condo. I sat to watch for them and they paused at the chairs for a short rest. Later, as I retrieved the chairs, I found the mother had written a simple message in the sand, Thank you. I thought what a great opportunity this had been for me to meet them. I never learned their names, but I will remember them forever.

As I stood there, reading that simple message, I thought that if I could work with the same persistence and determination shown by this deaf and blind lady, coupled with my good health, anything and everything would be possible. A sense of humility filled me as I looked at the footprints left in the sand. What a lesson. I often think of the two women and this day when I need a boost. We often need to pinch ourselves to remind us just how good life is. It is how you look at each day as to how you will spend it. Make the best of each day and you will experience happiness in the majority of them.

I have seen that those who are persistent, those who keep trying after others have quit are the ones who will find success. Persistence and determination are the driving forces to success. The amount of persistence you show will be a direct measure of the faith you have in yourself. The majority of men who suffer failure do so due to their lack of faith to fuel their determination. Often they find later that success was within their grasp if only they had endured the struggle a little longer. The extra effort to find another approach or a different view is often the secret to success.

The enthusiasm you use continues to drive you towards the goal and will give an added effectiveness to reach the winner's circle. **Persistence and determination are essential factors found in the character of successful men and women.**

Nothing In This World
Can Take the Place of Persistence

A quote by President Calvin Coolidge is one of the best ever on this subject. **"Nothing in this world can take the place of persistence. Talent will not; nothing is more common than unsuccessful people with talent. Genius will not; unrewarded genius is almost a proverb. Education will not; the world is full of educated derelicts. Persistence and determination alone are omnipotent. The slogan "press on" has solved and always will solve the problems of the human race."**

Chapter Fifteen

The Power of Desire

What You May Lack in Talent Can Be Offset With Desire and Drive

"We accomplish things by directing our desires, not by ignoring them."
Author Unknown

We often hear about how being a Shriner makes good men better. A couple of years ago, I attended the Florida Shrine Association Convention in Fort Myers, Florida. While there I saw a true example of the desire to excel and succeed during one of the competitions. It was a pleasure to witness. I saw action that made me proud to be a member of the Shriners organization. It was very enjoyable to watch how a young man handled a difficult situation. He had the desire in his heart to do his best, and that is exactly what he did.

A hot day in the middle of a Fort Myers parking lot with temperatures approaching 90 degrees had everyone yearning for a cool drink. The events that day were the competition for the Florida Shrine Motor Corps. Mini bikes, fancy Harley Davidson motorcycles, Tin Lizzies, go carts and other types of vehicles were entered in competition for trophies.

One of the premier events involved the large Harley Davidson motorcycles in an obstacle course. These riders appear to maneuver these large bikes through this tightly laid out course as if they could do it in their sleep. Don't be fooled, riding through this course takes concentration, athletic ability, skill, practice, and maybe a little bit of luck to get the best time and the trophy. You can see their nervousness and the anticipation eating at them, they always have the fear of messing up, getting to aggressive and not making it through the course. If this happens, then that is it, see you in next years competition.

As a young man in his twenties pulled up to the starting line, you could see the desire and determination on his face. He was no doubt a contender for the best time of the day. Everyone knew it, but that only seems to put more pressure on someone when you are expected to do well. As he squealed the tires off the starting line and headed down the course everyone was watching, he made that first turn perfectly. It seemed that his body and the bike were one working in unison as he glides thru the course making the difficult look almost like music in motion.

As he approached the finish line it soon became apparent that this young man was going to have a flawless ride and turn in the best time of the day, so far. He hit the finish line with a smile on his face, and that look of pleasure and confidence that you get when you know that you have done something extremely well. A man standing next to me who was timing the run on his personal stop watch held it up to me to confirm that this was, in fact, the best time of the day. It was an exciting moment to see how this young mans desire to succeed had become a reality.

For some unknown reason, the official clock did not record his time. The judges determined the rider would have to run the course again. I thought to myself putting two runs together back to back would be almost impossible. If this happened to me, I think I would have lost it. Even if I could have kept my composure, how could I concentrate enough to make the run again?

As they broke the news to this young man, I could see his smile turn to disappointment; you could see in his body language that he was concerned about rerunning the course again. To my amazement his confidence again began to quickly shine through, **it was a true sign of his deep desire to succeed.** There was never one solitary bad word spoken, he blamed no one, he handled it like a man, probably much better than anyone that was watching.

He pulled up to that starting line to give it his best shot once again. A sense of pride puffed up in my chest, to see this young guy handle himself so wonderfully under this most difficult situation. As he ran the course this time, there were cheers from everyone, as everyone now was a part of this young man's team. This is where the real test of an individual has an opportunity to shine through. This is where the true meaning of the statement "the Shrine makes a good man better" has a chance to prove itself.

As this rider made his way a second time around this challenging course, he proved to me without a doubt, the Shrine of North America does exactly that, it makes good men better. This rider did the unthinkable, he rode the course twice, and twice he turned in the best time of the day. As the day progressed and ended his time stood as the best, and earned him first place on this day. This proved to me that if you greatly desire something, you will find the guts and the stamina to make it come true regardless of the obstacles you have to overcome.

When you talk about competition, a name such as Mario Andretti, Champion Race Car Driver, would be among the first to be mentioned. On the racing circuit few men have equaled Andretti's prowess. Mario once said, **"Desire is the key to motivation, it's the determination and commitment to an unrelenting pursuit of your goal – a commitment to excellence – that will enable you to attain the success you seek."** Desire is the key to everything we hope and dream about, for it is desire that creates the power.

Often it is not the most talented, or educated, or skilled that crosses the finish line first. The person with a burning desire within him will find a way to do his best with what talent he has to take the chance for victory. Staying power or stamina comes from desire built with enthusiasm and commitment. William Shakespeare said, **"Is it not strange that desire should so many years outlive performance."** It was true when he said it, and it is true now.

Is It Not Strange That Desire Should So Many Years Outlive Performance

Desire is found in athletics, some athletes burning desire reaches far beyond the normal player. I can think of no better place than a NBA Basketball court to make the case for desire working at its best. As a season ticket holder of the Orlando Magic, I enjoy watching basketball; and especially enjoy watching players who give it their all.

The Magic have fielded some great players, but one player who wore the number 4, Scott Skiles, was the icon for the word competitor. Often the smallest player, never the fastest player, or the most talented and he seldom seemed to get the lucky break. Still he played each game with such relentless desire it became contagious to his teammates on the floor. Alone his inner desire gave him the ability to take the entire team to a higher level.

He played unselfishly for the team and this was proven December 30, 1990 when he set the NBA record with 30 assist. This record stands today. I watched that game and the record was earned for one reason, desire. Scott educated each of the 17,000 fans on the true meaning of **what you lack in talent; you can make up with desire and hustle if you give it all you have.**

In my experience I have found desire to be one of the key ingredients in the recipe for building a successful life. No matter what you hope or how big your dreams are; you must find the desire to give you the strength to finish what ever task you select or you may never find success. We can achieve greatness if we follow our desires. Our desires influenced by our hopes and dreams guide us to our future.

"Champions aren't made in gyms. Champions are made from something they have deep inside them – a desire, a dream, a vision. They have to have last minute stamina, they have to be a little faster, they have to have the skill and the will. But the will must be stronger than the skill" **Muhammad Ali, World Heavyweight Boxing Champion. (61 pro fights, 56 wins, 37 KOs, 5 lost, 1 by KO)**

Chapter Sixteen

The Power of A Compliment

Praise and Recognition of Others Should Become an Everyday Item on Your Agenda

"Praise invariably implies a reference to a higher standard." **Aristotle**

Compliments! We all love to receive them. A few nice words can make you feel like you are on cloud nine. A nice compliment is what you need to keep going. It can warm your heart and make your day sparkle. A pat on the back, a heartfelt compliment, or a sign of appreciation can make a person feel good. Knowing how effective compliments can be, it is equally amazing to me how few people actually give them to others. Communicating to another how proud you are of them or how much you appreciate what they have accomplished cost you nothing more than a sincere compliment.

Often we underestimate the power or the good will that comes from a kind word. I see people criticize another for a minor mistake, when an honest compliment would be the best way to handle a problem. Through just the slightest of gestures you can compliment others on doing a good job. **A word of encouragement during a failure is worth more than an hour of praise after a success.**

Compliments build morale, teamwork, and bring out the best in others. Words of appreciation are powerful and productive words you use to build relationships for the future. A young child complimented for doing a good job responds with smiles and a prideful lift of their heads. Understanding how much a child appreciates a compliment and seeing how influential it can be on their young lives should inspire everyone to compliment them daily.

I have a friend who has made a mission of giving compliments to always let others know when they have excelled in a task. I know people appreciate his sincere praise, along with his "Thank you for what you have done" message. He has taken complimenting others to another level by making it a point to also let a persons spouse and family also know how he feels. I have often seen him telling a lady how proud he is of her husband. Then he turns it up another notch by telling the lady how much he appreciates her support for her husband, and he thanks her for allowing her husband to live out his dreams.

What is accomplished by my friend's way of letting a person's family know how proud he is of them? First, it reinforces his honest sincerity. Second, it allows others who are close to the person you complimented to know how well he is doing. Third, it opens the door for family member's future support to continue on his mission. Finally, it is a powerful tool especially in a volunteer organization where praise and respect are the only pay.

Compliments must be given with sincerity. A statement of praise taken as cheap flattery will never have the same effect and may even be detrimental. The following are essential keys, I found to enhance the quality of a compliment:

Appreciation
Genuine Praise
Heartfelt Thanks
Ask for an Opinion
Sincerity in Delivery
Trustworthy Relationship

Compliments are given in many forms. The best way is to deliver the compliment to an individual before a group of his peers or his superiors. The face to face praise is always a positive method. Another excellent vehicle is though a written note or thank you card. Many consider the written compliment to be the best tactic as it can be saved and cherished forever. Often people frame and display it for all to see. Someone can cherish a note that cost nothing simply because of the written words or they consider it valuable because a special person complimented them. The results gained from the praise of others for their efforts should inspire everyone.

Another form of a compliment is when you are asked for an opinion. It encourages people to know that others trust and value their thoughts on how to solve projects and problems. It is equally satisfying to have them listen attentively to your answers. Trust is one of the highest forms of compliment. It is said that trust is greater even than love when it come to compliments.

Have you ever wondered what keeps people excited, motivated and eager to be helpful in a volunteer organization, at work, at your church or even within your family? How some leaders in all venues of life have all of the cheerful help they need? And for others, help is so scarce they often end up doing the work themselves?

One compliment
Can keep me going
For a whole month.

Success is directly related to the positive influence and personal recognition given to those who work around you. A simple compliment, a thank you, and the ability to let a person know how much you appreciate the work they are doing makes the difference. Every person enjoys being appreciated for what he does, and gives them the fuel needed to accomplish more. Mark Twain said, **"One compliment can keep me going for a whole month."** As easy as it sounds many leaders fail in this simple task, and in return lose the support of the many waiting to be recognized and asked to help with the next project.

To get the most support from everyone, treat them all as if they were a 10. If they believe they are a 10 in your book, they will try to live up to that level. Think about it, you had a teacher, coach, or friend who always believed you were outstanding. Didn't you always give the extra effort to keep his faith? Your ability to perform for a person that is convinced you are perfect is always better than for a person who treats you as a stepchild. Build positive relationships that result in people working as a team to get the job done. People who value and respect one another enjoy their time together and as a result follow and support their leader. All this can be accomplished with an occasional simple complement or a sincere thank you for someone who deserves it.

You might ask where do I begin. Find a colleague who deserves a "well done." Make it a goal to give three compliments each day to people at work. Follow it with a minimum of three sincere "thank you" to people that have helped make your day better. As a leader, you should provide constant recognition for those who work for you. A simple solution is naming a Worker of the Month, or giving a small special gift, or mailing five thank you cards each month. Can you remember the last time you received an unexpected thank you card in the mail? How did it make you feel? Think of the support group you could build by simply making those around you feel appreciated and needed. Try it. Begin building your team of 10's now, and as a leader you will have continual support and help.

We gain the success we want through the support and help of others by complimenting them. We must thank everyone to make them feel appreciated and needed, and this contributes to our own accomplishments. When we synchronize our efforts with everyone around us then our goals become attainable. This maxim holds true in every aspect of life. Make it a point to compliment others.

Compliments have been part of the American life since the beginning. They encourage and motivate others to do their best and give appreciation to those who have already given their all. In his closing remarks at the Sanitary Fair in Washington D.C. on March 18, 1864 as the Civil War was being fought,

President Abraham Lincoln had this to say.
"I have never studied the art of paying compliments to women, but I must say that if all that has been said by orators and poets since the creation of the world in praise of women were applied to the women of America, it would not do them justice for their conduct during this war. I will close by saying, God bless the women of America!"

Chapter Seventeen

Become A Mentor and A Coach

Good Leaders Help Others to Reach For And Attain Their Personal Best

"The achievements of an organization are the result of the combined effort of each individual." **Vince Lombardi**

My childhood in Wisconsin spanned the late 50's and 60's where if you loved sports it was the Green Bay Packer era. As a young boy when some person said coach, the next word would be Lombardi. Vince

Lombardi was a coach held in the highest regards by friend and foe. The Super Bowl Trophy bears his name. While I never met Coach Lombardi, he was my favorite coach and as most boys my age in Wisconsin felt as if I knew him. We would see him on the sidelines during the game moving up and down encouraging and **coaching.** The television on Sunday afternoon always featured him striving to coach the Packers to victory. Coach Lombardi undoubtedly ranks as a great coach by winning 2 Super Bowls and 5 NFL Championship, but as great as his effect on his team and football in general he was the hallmark of a good coach to thousands of young men across the nation.

Lombardi quotes were tossed around by the media and the youngsters as if they were proclamations from the Oracle at Delphi. Dozens of quotes float around in the cosmic ether, but two mark the basis of this great man's mind. "The quality of a person's life is in direct proportion to their commitment to excellence, regardless of their chosen field of endeavor." **"The price of success is hard work, dedication to the job at hand, and the determination that whether we win or lose, we have applied the best of ourselves to the task at hand."**

The Quality Of A Person's Life Is In Direct Proportion To Their Commitment To Excellence

Performing as a great coach requires unconditional commitment to your team. This carries over to all aspects of life, not just the sports arena. Today, someone who leads in the business world can be viewed as a coach within his area of expertise. Being a coach in the work place puts you in a position of helping others to achieve their personal best.

Over the years I have known men and women, at times even unknown to themselves, who are coaching others. Having that innate ability to help others by leading or coaching them to reach a higher level is a talent you have to develop with practice to become consistent. A great coach has the quality of teaching another not only to do a job correctly, but to do it on their own. Great coaches without exception teach, inspire, and motivate others to expect excellence in all their endeavors. Another thought from my favorite Coach, "**A man can be as great as he wants to be. If you believe in yourself and have the courage, the determination, the dedication, the competitive drive and if you are willing to sacrifice the little things in life and pay the price for the things worthwhile, it can be done.**" Coach Lombardi was a great coach. Many of his quotes can be used in the business world as well as in the sports world. Here he is basically saying, give up the little things and strive for the big things in life.

Mentors play important roles in many business organizations in the world. Mentors usually work one on one with the more experienced mentor guiding a new colleague along the way. Mentors check progress from time to time, avail themselves to instruct or answer questions, and to help you find opportunities. A good mentor will help insure success and use their experience to help guide your career.

Mentors are found in civic and fraternal organizations as well as in business. Organizations use mentors to help in the orientation of new members. A good mentoring relationship will build a comfort zone for the new associate to make them eager to become involved in new activities. Mentoring focuses on the individual and thereby enhances morale, motivation, and participation in organizational programs.

Although the coach's role is similar to a mentors, the coach is usually involved with a group or team. Coaches not only must teach but also lead, inspire, and motivate the group to become a cohesive unit in order for the team to perform at a high level. Coaching is a full time job wither you are involve with a sports team, a business group, or a voluntary organization. The term full time does not mean round the clock but that you are committed fully during a set period of time. George Halas, long time coach of the Chicago Bears' NFL team, was asked what makes a good coach? He replied simply, **"Complete dedication."**

The ability to coach others is essential to become a great leader. Hard work and dedication are required to inspire others to follow. I want to list some of the characteristics needed to become a good coach within your area of expertise:

Be Persistent
Communicate
Be Committed
Believe in Others
Empower Others
Motivate & Inspire
Be a Good Listener
Teach Understanding
Coach, Don't Control
Guide to Independence

To be a good coach or leader, you have to understand the meaning of the word, limitation. At work, you want your workers to be first class, but often this is not the case. Early in my career, I told my boss that many people working under me did not seem to functioning at their full potential. I was frustrated and felt ineffective.

He knew I tried hard to bring out the best in my crew and was sympathetic. He asked about my school days. "When you were in school did everyone get all A's? Do you think everyone was capable of getting all A's? Maybe those getting B's and C's were doing the best they could. Possibly some student could have done better, but for others the B or C was excellent.

Good Leaders Will Work And Coach Others To Be Their Personal Best

Understand not everyone can be an A student. As a leader, you must adjust and place individuals into positions that stretch them, but not embarrass them. Good leaders will work and coach others to their personal best whatever level that may be." I try to use this good leader's advice daily.

Paul "Bear" Bryant, best know as the football coach of the University of Alabama's Crimson Tide. The winningest coach in NCAA Division history with 323 victories to 85 losses and 17 ties got his nickname "Bear" from wrestling a bear at a carnival. His teams won football games because he understood men.

When asked how he rated players, he revealed that there were three types. **"First, there are those who are winners and know they are winners. Then there are the losers who know they are losers. Then there are those who are not winners but don't know it. They're the ones for me. They never quit trying. They're the soul of our game. In order to have a winner, the team must have a feeling of unity;**

every player must put the team first --- ahead of personal glory."

People may forget what you say, or forget what you do, but will always remember how you make them feel

Chapter Eighteen

Making Your Dreams Become Reality

Free Your Mind, All Dreams Can Be Made Real
If You Have the Courage and Drive to Pursue Them

The only limit to our realization of tomorrow
will be our doubts of today.
Franklin Delano Roosevelt

D reams and dreaming are one important way to look at possible ways to improve ourselves and the world around us. Dreaming is a process where there are no restrictions, the sky is the limit, and even that is unlimited when you dream. Dreaming gives a person the opportunity to see things as we would wish they were.

Everything in the world began as a dream in someone's mind. Today we do what was impossible just a few short years ago. We are living the fantasies of yesteryear's science fiction films routinely doing things that were only thoughts half a century ago. Walt Disney said, **"All of our dreams can come true, if we have the courage to pursue them."**

All of us dream, but few make their dreams reality to share with others. Some dreamers' dreams without action, while others take their dreams add commitment and effort to make the dream come true. Your dream might be for better family relationships, or a dream of a new product or process, or it might even be a dream which would change the world.

Take a moment to think of dreams in someone's mind that changed the world. A scant 60 years ago, a computer filled rooms while today you hold it on you lap. The idea of a cell phone that could send pictures, text, or the voice around the world without wire began in someone's fertile imagination. **"The human voice carries entirely too far as it is...and now you fellows come along and seek to complicate matters."** Such were Mark Twain's thoughts on hearing about the original telephone. What would he say if he were here today?"

Advancements in the medical worlds are made daily. Days, months, years are being added to a person's life expectancy. Sometimes things happen by accident, but more often events come about through a person's dreams, their preparation, and the ability to see the results in their own mind. These people are the energy and the commitment to see the task to completion. Still, it all starts with a dream inside someone's brain. Dreams honor the past, embrace the present and shape the future.

A great thing about dreams is that they are free. Only turning the dream into reality cost the dreamer time, effort, and commitment. Dream, dream, and dream some more; you might dream the answer to tomorrow's question. When it comes to making dreams come true, I like what President Harry Truman said, **"I studied the lives of great men and famous women, and I found that the men and women who got to the top were those who did the job at hand, with everything they had of energy and enthusiasm."**

Each year selected schools in Central Florida nominate a student to receive the **Walt Disney's Dreamer and Doer Award."** This wonderful award encourages young children to dream, a trail Walt Disney himself exhibited. Walt stated, "Somehow I can't believe there are any heights that can't be scaled by a man who knows the secret of making dreams come true. This special secret, it seems to me, can be summarized in four C's. They are Curiosity, Confidence, Courage, and Constancy and the greatest of these is Confidence. When you believe a thing, believe it all the way, implicitly and unquestionably." The four C's are used as a guide in selecting each recipient of the award. Faculties select students who are most likely to follow in Walt's footsteps that will dream and work to make those dreams reality. Winners received an award and are invite to spend a day at Disney World accompanied by their families.

Several years ago, my daughter, Lisa, received the Dreamer and Doer Award. Her passionate dreams concerned playing basketball at a high standard. Her passion and effort made the dream come true as she was named captain of her college team and played in a national tournament. After her final college game I sent her this note:

Lisa,

Your dream started at the age of eight when you and I would regularly attend the Orlando Magic games. You fell in love with the game, and soon basketball became a good bond between us. In High School you played with determination, and as the leader of your team you were selected as the team captain. Your hard work and commitment to the game along with your excellent grades earned you a full scholarship to play basketball through college. I could not have been prouder.

As you know this dream was not easy, two serious car accidents, either one of which could have taken your life slowed your ability to play. Though frustrated at times, you were relentless in your commitment to be a good basketball player. Finally in your senior year you were healthy and at full strength. Again because of your commitment and leadership skills her teammates selected you as the captain of the team. As you know this team became known at your school as the team of first, the first team in school history to win their conference, to win the Florida tournament, and the first to reach the National NAIA Championship Tournament. What an honor for you and all the girls on the team to reach this level.

Your dream turned out to be a tremendous trip for you and me. What a way to end your basketball career. I could have never imagined when you were that little 8 year old daughter of mine and you told me at a Magic game that you wanted to play basketball it would end up being a story like this. Fourteen years later and here we

are, after a lot of sweat and tears, playing your final collegiate game in the National Championship Tournament, something so few have ever accomplished. The whole experience has been a Dream come true for not only you Lisa, but for myself as well. A win would have been nice in the championship game, but the trip has been awesome, I know I could not be prouder of you. Thank you for including me in your dreams.

Keep Dreaming,
Dad

Her basketball dream brought other benefits besides the competition. She traveled, made lifetime friendships and learned the exhilaration of winning and the balancing pain to accept defeat. One day at the Sportsplex in Orlando, she had the opportunity to play in a "pick up" game. One of her team mates was Julius "Dr. J" Erving, a great professional player. Can you imagine her feeling to be playing alongside one of the greats of the game? Dreams...... they will take you to places you can not begin to envision.

Remember All Things Are Possible For Those Individuals That Believe

You realize nothing happens unless there is a dream. The dream may seem impossible, and then with further thought it becomes unlikely. The "now" generation is in conflict with the "yesterday" generation because they know no fear. With work and commitment it may soon look to be probable, finally through persistence you reach the realm of the dream becoming reality. It happens when you are committed to keep your dreams alive.

Age unfortunately affects our vision; we begin to see why things will not work versus why they could. Having six children ranging from 19 to 29, our home is a reservoir of dreams and ideas. The effect on Anne and me is akin to being plunged into an anti-aging solution. It is invigorating to be immersed in the ideas that bubble up from these young persons. I find myself trying to hold them back at times, but that seems to only strengthen their will. Each is on a mission to fulfill their dreams, working without fear and with commitment and passion. We have to remember history is only memory; dreams are the vehicle to the future. The only thing that can stop your dreams is you.

George Bernard Shaw captured dreams becoming reality with a simple statement, **"Some men see things as they are and say, "Why?" I dream of things that never were and say, "Why not?"**

> **"Some men see things as**
> **They are and say, "Why?"**
> **I dream of things that**
> **Never were and say,**
> **"Why not?"**

I recently heard a story about the day Disney World opened up in Orlando. It relates itself to dreams and visions and how they move onto reality. Walt Disney was involved in the everyday designing and creation of the world premier theme park, however he passed away prior to the first patron attending. On opening day Lillian, his wife greeted people as they entered the park for the first time. Many people said to her, "Don't you wish Walt could have seen this place." Her reply was always the same, **"Walt saw this park long ago, it was his dream, he had a vision of exactly how it would look."**

"He who multiplies riches multiplies cares."

Benjamin Franklin

Chapter Nineteen

The Greatest Asset of All

Do You Know Where to Find It?
Who Holds the Key to Your Greatest Asset?

Have you ever considered what your greatest personal asset is? I travel the country and whenever I ask that question I receive a puzzled look. It is a simple question, yet the answer never seems to be simple. In a group, you will receive myriad answers.

When asked about an asset, people consider material assets first. Homes, cars, businesses, and savings accounts come to mind. Most are reluctant to talk about that type of asset with a stranger. So as they search for an answer, they begin to realize their most important assets are not the material ones. Now they retreat into deep thought over the question. One would think something this important would be on the tip of their tongue, but seldom is.

Some of the better answers are time, health, or children. The list goes on of business, customers, friends, ad infinitum. All these responses are better than material assets.

I believe everyone's greatest asset is themselves. You alone are responsible for your life. It might sound egotistical; but keep it in the right context. We are talking about personal assets. Every person determines their own destiny through their actions. You determine if your personal conduct to employees, fellow workers, or customers will be acceptable. Character rises and falls on how you handle yourself in different situations.

To often the lack of success is blamed on another for not doing their part. You and you alone are in control of your destiny; blame it on no one else. To me that makes you your greatest personal asset. Bear in mind success is not normally achieved alone, but if we use the tools and people skills we are blessed with, then we will never be alone.

To take this a step further, in the corporate world the company's greatest asset is not any one person; it is the people, the workforce. It is not a product or company history that makes a great company for a company is only as good as the people it keeps.

How People Are Treated And How Well They Do, Is A Reflection Of How Happy They Are.

The natural progression would move to the nation and beyond. In the final analysis the answer is always the people.

Nothing is accomplished without the people. They are the greatest asset on earth, and should be treated as such. In this book we have looked at ways to improve ourselves as we **Campaign for a Better Life.** It should be clear to achieve the fullest in life our focus must always be on those around us.

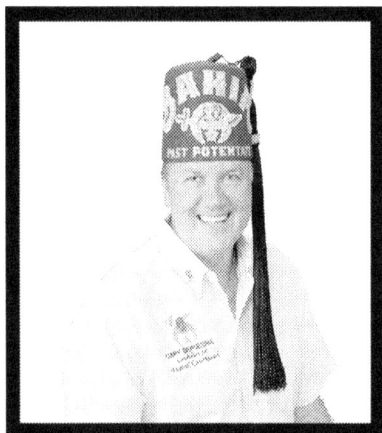

During 2006 as I campaigned for an International office with the Shriners, I ended my presentations with the following. It can be modified to fit any organization with just a few adjustments in content.

In Closing I Would Like To Leave You With This

What is the greatest asset of the Shrine of North America? I know that earlier in my talk we have mentioned areas we need to work on, but very seldom do we ever talk about the Shrines greatest asset.

I can tell you that it is not our rich heritage and many famous former members, and I can tell you that it is not our current top leaders.

Some of you might be surprised to hear me say that it is not our large endowment fund and that our greatest asset is not our 22 Shriners Hospitals for Children.

You see an organizations greatest asset, is determined to be, the one, that if taken away, all else is lost. That is such an important statement; allow me to say it again.

An organizations greatest asset,
Is determined to be, the one,
That if taken away,
All else is lost.

And so, in my mind the greatest asset of the Shrine of North America is...... Its people, its 400,000 members who give of their time and their talents to ensure this fraternity will prosper into the future. Thank you to each of you for all that you do, and will continue to do in the future for this fraternity.

If you are your greatest personal asset then it becomes paramount you maintain and magnify it. Reading is a premiere method of doing just that. Include in you schedule time to read and read books that expands your knowledge. Set a personal goal of reading a book every week, or one every month, whatever your schedule will allow. Walt Disney said, **"There is more treasure in books than in all the pirates loot on Treasure Island and best of all, you can enjoy these riches every day of your life."** So read and continue to build your greatest asset, you.

Chapter Twenty

Modernize For
A Better Future

Accepting Change Leads to Modernization
Allowing Your Move into the Future
With Greater Ease and Success

"We grow great by dreams.
All big men are dreamers." **Woodrow Wilson**

A man opens the front door as his wife pulls into the driveway. Walking to the door, she gives him a kiss and says, "I love you honey, how was your day?" He replies, "I came home early and decided to change all the furniture in the house." "Change, change," she says. "How could you change anything without my being a part of it?" The word "change" puts her on the defensive, thoughts of unwanted change fills her mind and it becomes clear there is a problem. The husband realizes he has made a mistake. Often change is not accepted easily.

I do not like the word for too many people read the wrong meaning into the word. Some will resist before they even know what the change is. Change means moving from the comfortable now to an uncomfortable possibility. Change, even for the better, is always accompanied by drawbacks and discomforts. The challenge is to overcome the fear of change and to embrace it.

I avoid using the word because it always seems to carry with it friction or resentment. I substitute the word "modernize" to let the people understand we are getting ahead or doing something in a better way. In our story, if the husband told his wife that he had spent the afternoon modernizing the house to make things easier on her, the response would have been totally different. She would have viewed the change with hope and curiosity. In the end, she may not have liked the result, but her mind would have been open not closed from the beginning.

Try Replacing the Word Modernize
For the Word Change

Try it, by simply inserting the word modernize in place of change it will make a difference. No matter the type of business you have or if you have done well in the past, if you are to continue to be successful you must change. I mean, you must modernize. President John F. Kennedy said, "Change is the law of life. And those who look only to the past or present are certain to miss the future."

"Change is the law of life. And those who look only to the past or present are certain to miss the future."

Modernizing or changing if you will, is necessary to keep you even or ahead of the competition. Never fear trying something new or to take the chance to develop a new project you believe in. Only those who do nothing make no mistakes. An old cliché goes, "It was amateurs that built the Ark and professionals that built the Titanic." Modernizing is much like dreaming, often if you can visualize it, you can achieve it. President Franklin D. Roosevelt had this take on the subject. **"It is common sense to take a method and try it. If it fails, admit it frankly and try another. But above all, try something."**

How fast things are changing hit home last year when I received and email from an elderly friend. Although in his 80's, he remained alert and involved in the events of the day. His computer was his window to the world which kept him connected. The following is a small clip of one of his last emails:

It has been a rough year for me. I can only walk about 30 feet, then, I'm exhausted and out of breath. This congestive heart failure, emphysema, and diabetes are about to get me. It won't be long I know. I am trying my best to keep going. I don't worry about the future; I just hate to miss so many of the new technical

improvements and inventions that will come out in the next few years. God bless you, and yours, and your efforts. I thank you for all you have done.

The message hit me hard, but impressed me about how fast things are changing. His main concern was not about death, he could deal with that. He had gone from fabric covered biplanes to 747 jumbo jets in his lifetime. His regret was not seeing the **changes** that would come in the next 80 years. This should make us all appreciative of the times we live in where improvements happen daily.

What determines the future? You determine the future. Your future will be gauged by your ability to maintain pace with that change. At times you have to not only ask yourself if you are changing, but have to ask if you are changing fast enough to keep up. The world is changing or modernizing faster than ever before. Today, we live in a world where change is not only probable, it is inevitable and continuous. The need to keep up with change is vital to our survival, especially at high levels of corporations, and in our national government. Still, even with this, the world hates change, but it is the only process that has brought us progress. President John F. Kennedy said, **"We should not let fears hold us back from pursuing our hopes."**

Let's now take a moment to look at how to create change, wither it is a personal change, or a company change, or a change within your family. First and foremost, determine if a change is what is best. If you do not like something, change it, if you can not change it, then change the way you react to it. The result should be better than where you started. Probably the most important aspect you need is a positive attitude to maintain focus while working towards change. Negative attitudes will destroy a successful completion.

Open your mind to visions and dreams and you will move forward to positive changes. The willingness to change shows strength of character of whoever tries to make things better through their efforts. It is inconceivable to consider a future without change. You must realize when you are through changing, you are though.

If you want life to be different, you must modernize to today's standards. It is never too late to become what you dreamed you could be. It only takes the commitment to begin. Change your manner of thinking and your world will change around you. If you truly want your life to be different, the force will come from within. You alone can make it happen. This book offers you the tools to begin to build that different life. It will only take modernizing your skills and talents.

"God grant me the serenity to accept the people I cannot change, the courage to change the ones I can and the wisdom to change myself." **Author Unknown**

Gary Bergenske

Conclusion

Here we are, at the end of the book. I feel great about you giving me the opportunity to share these **20 chapters** that give you the tools to change your life. I believe they will if you use them, because I have been practicing all of them for many years. I also know that often when so much information is given to you all at once there is a tendency to lose some of it. Here is what I would ask of you as you **Campaign for a better life:**

1. Make the commitment to follow through on personally developing these tools.

2. You should do everything with character and integrity.

3. Believe in what you are doing. Be determined and persistent.

4. Selecting at least two tools per week you will concentrate on.

5. Be contagious, bring others with you on this success trip.

6. Make enthusiasm and charisma part of your everyday life.

7. Don't be afraid to think out of the box, and I mean way out.

8. Constantly work on your communication skills, all of them.

9. Remember to always compliment others, they will respect you for it.

10. Think Modernize, and remember you are your greatest personal asset.

As you work on following these suggestions you will soon find your life changing. You will begin to feel a sense of pride in what you are doing. Before long others will be looking up to you for ideas and advice. The more you work at it the better you will become, and the more natural it will feel. I have worked with many leaders over the years at many different levels. One thing I have found to be true with all leaders regardless of where they are on the totem pole, they still strive for more. I find great leaders always strive to improve themselves as they become permanent students of improving their leadership skills. In doing so, they improve everyone around them, and as a group they can all go to the next level.

Let the people of the world know that with the beginning of a new generation, the torch has been passed. Each new generation will have the ability to use their minds and schedule their time as no other generation preceding them has had the opportunity to do. The responsibility is in the hands of all of us to use our minds and time to the fullest, and to teach the children of the world to do the same. For in doing so, this world will become a better place for all of mankind.

I wish you the best, you deserve it. If you are a person that has taken the time to read this book, you are the type of person any great leader would love to have on his team. One that believes in improving them self and believes in helping others. May God bless you and your efforts in building a better life for yourself and those around you.

> *I hope that when my days are done,*
> *My achievements will be these;*
> *That I will have fought for what was right and*
> *fair for all, That I will have risked for that which*
> *mattered, and that I will have given to those who*
> *were in need of help. My goal is to leave this*
> *place a better place – to have Helped to make*
> *lives better for others by leading and*
> *Motivating them to be the best they can.*

Gary Bergenske

About the Author

Gary Bergenske was born in Madison, Wisconsin in 1954 and raised in Pardeeville, a small nearby town. After graduating from Portage High School, he and his family moved to Jacksonville, Florida. Never having attended college, Gary began his working life in restaurants and selling insurance for Northwestern Mutual, becoming one of their youngest million dollar sellers at the age of 21.

In 1985 he pursued his dream of owning his own business by purchasing J & J Metro Moving and Storage Co. in Orlando,

Florida. As the company President/Owner, three years later he purchased a competitors business. The company has continued to grow under Gary's leadership by purchasing an additional three competitors in Florida. Gary believes in leading others the same way he lives and manages his own life, with desire and passion. His success, although self motivated has been made with the help of others because of his talent to communicate ideas and goals. He has taken on a second calling in a mission to influence others in a positive way. His focus is in helping others reach their full leadership potential.

A motivational speaker, he has delivered his inspirational message on leadership, teamwork, and mentoring at engagements through out the United States. He served as Potentate of Bahia Shriners in Orlando, Florida in 2005 and is a dedicated supporter of Shriners Hospitals for Children.

Gary and Anne, his wife, have six children aged 19 to 29. The children, three boys and three girls that are often referred to as the Bergy Bunch. The family maintains a vacation home on Daytona Beach. Gary loves and collects antique automobiles but his favorite recreational vehicle is his Harley Davidson.

Gary Bergenske is available for speaking engagements and personal appearances. For more information contact:

Gary Bergenske
1101 West Kennedy Boulevard
Orlando, Florida   32810

Phone: 407-875-0000
FAX: 407-875-0480
GBergenske@aol.com

Visit Gary Bergenske's Web site at
www.Garymotivations.com
or
www.ShrinerGary.com

To purchase additional copies of "**Campaign for a Better Life**" contact your favorite bookstore or go online to www.Campaignforabetterlife.com or by faxing your order to (407) 875-0480.

Advantage
BOOKS & MUSIC

Longwood, Florida, USA
"we bring dreams to life"™
www.advbooks.com

You can contact
Gary Bergenske at:
GBergenske@aol.com

www.GaryMotivations.com

GARY BERGENSKE
Motivations